EXPLORING CAREERS
AS A
COMPUTER TECHNICIAN

By

Jean W. Spencer

THE ROSEN PUBLISHING GROUP

NEW YORK

Published in 1985 by The Rosen Publishing Group, Inc.
29 East 21st Street, New York City, New York 10010

First Edition
Copyright 1985 by Jean Spencer

Library of Congress Cataloging in Publication Data

Spencer, Jean W.
  Exploring careers as a computer technician.

  1. Electronic digital computers—Vocational guidance.
2. Electronic data processing—Vocational guidance.
I. Title.
QA76.25.S66   1984   001.64′023   84–6977
ISBN 0-8239-0626-4

EXPLORING CAREERS
AS A
COMPUTER TECHNICIAN

To
John M. Spencer,
significant technician,
and
Ross R. Olney
with
appreciation

About the Author

Jean W. Spencer is the Public Information Officer for Oxnard College and a member of the California Association of Community Colleges' Commission on Public Information, the Ventura County Public Information Communication Association, and ComputerTown Inc. A long-time reporter, feature writer, poet, and free-lance writer-photographer, she has been published by more than a dozen newspapers (including the Philadelphia *Bulletin*) on both coasts and more than two dozen national magazines and books. A graduate of Ventura College, she also attended Charles Morris Price School of Advertising and Journalism on an academic scholarship. She is an ordained elder in the Presbyterian Church and a lay leader for Faith at Work, Inc., and has been honored as an Outstanding Young Woman of America for civic and philanthropic involvement. She is a computer enthusiast and computer literacy advocate.

Acknowledgments

Special thanks are in order for the many individuals, companies, and organizations that contributed to the substance of this book. Their overwhelming contributions are, of course, to the Information Age that is now upon us. I am grateful for the time, knowledge, and interest shared by:

Apple Computer Co.
Computer and Business Equipment Manufacturers Association
American Association of Engineering Societies
Society of Manufacturing Engineers
U.S. Department of Labor
California Employment Development Department
American Federation of Information Processing Societies
California State Department of Education
TRW
U.S. Air Force
ComputerTown Inc.
DeVry Institute of Technology
Bell and Howell Education Group
NRI/McGraw-Hill Continuing Education
Vocational Studies Center, University of Wisconsin
Cleveland Institute of Electronics
Mt. San Antonio College
San Jose Community College District
Evergreen Valley College
Los Angeles Harbor College
Digital Equipment Corporation
Wang
Radio Shack/Tandy
Jensen Tools
Sperry Univac
Honeywell, Inc.
Sorbus
Institute of Electrical and Electronic Engineers

Association for Systems Management
Data Processing Management Association
Ventura County Community College District
Heathkit/Zenith
Computerland
Contact East

Also, Jerry Dywasuk, Mary Catherine Powers, Sharilyn A. Shampine, Rod Franz, Dale Ackerman, Tanya Burke, Dr. Ruth Hemming, Dr. Diane Moore, Ron Jackson, Allan Signor, Tom Castenada, Lee Nagel, Marvin Lane, Chris Melton, and significant others whose encouraging words are appreciated.

Contents

I.   *Careers in the Wonderful World of Computers*   1

II.   *Job Prospects*   7

III.   *What Does a Computer Technician Do?*   16

IV.   *Are You a Good Candidate?*   31

V.   *Education and Training*   35

VI.   *What Do You Need to Know?*   44

VII.   *Other Pathways to Your Goal*   51

VIII.   *How to Test Yourself*   56

IX.   *Opportunities for Women*   62

X.   *Equipment, Tools, and Computer Environments*   68

XI.   *Job-finding Techniques*   76

XII.   *Advancement and Job Satisfactions*   84

Appendix A: Colleges and Schools   93
Appendix B: Helpful Organizations   99
Appendix C: Publications   101
Appendix D: Glossary   103

EXPLORING CAREERS
AS A
COMPUTER TECHNICIAN

Chapter 1

Careers in the Wonderful World of Computers

There is a word for people who think that electronic computers are exciting and that computers will have much to do with shaping the world in the 1980's, 1990's, and beyond. That word is futurist.

A futurist is someone who looks ahead in time and begins to realize the direction in which the world is moving. A futurist also plans to be involved in the exciting new ventures that will shape the coming world. The futurist wants to be where the action is, to be part of that action, and, therefore, is willing and eager to explore new ideas.

That is why so many men and women, boys and girls, are thinking about computers and computer careers. Both adults and young people can be futurists. The key factor is that they are looking ahead. They want to be a part of the important things that computers will accomplish for all people.

Computers and what they can do are interesting. That's a fact.

By using computers, people can manage and use great amounts of information. They can do things that have never been done before. They can accomplish more—and faster—than any person has been able to do before. In addition, computers are capable of performing many important functions more logically and in a more organized way.

Already we are seeing automatic tellers at banks, retail computer terminals instead of cash registers in stores, advertising mailings that address each receiver in a personal manner, and auto repair scopes that can discover car problems almost instantly. Computer systems play a vital role in our lives. They help us make telephone calls, receive paychecks on time, and reserve tickets for travel, hotels, and entertainment. That is only the beginning.

People who work with computers are even more interesting. Some interest us because they possess the brainpower to design and create computers. Others are interesting because they understand these wonderful machines and are able to keep them operating as they were meant to operate.

In the years to come, almost everyone will use computers as routinely as people use telephones or typewriters. Computers will be in every business and in almost every home. Students preparing for every type of career will need to study computers also in order to carry out the functions of those careers. That includes fields such as business, engineering, natural sciences, economics, medicine, and sales.

Young people who are looking ahead are beginning to think like futurists. For instance, you are probably starting to think about your career. After all, you know that schoolwork is only the beginning. You will want to earn money and be a part of society's work force. And of course you will want to choose a career that will be interesting and challenging as well as providing money for living.

Futurists Plan to Learn New Skills

If you are considering a computer career, you are a futurist.

Are you excited about the future? Do you like challenges? Do you like to work with your hands? Do you like to make things happen? Do you like to feel capable?

Specific skills are needed to make computers perform "miracles." You may already know that, and, somewhere inside of you, you may believe that you can become one of the skilled people who are contributing to the electronic computer's ability to change the world.

The computer field is the new frontier and is very exciting both to work in and to plan for. The whole field didn't even exist when your parents were planning their careers. Now it is opening up to you with a variety of specialized computer careers to choose from.

Operators, programmers, engineers, designers, researchers, supervisors, and instructors are all part of the sophisticated team of workers who are inventing and using computers.

But what do computer users do when the system goes down? That is a key question. And it points to a career you may want to consider. Think about this.

Who has the knowledge and the expertise to make that computer system function again? Who understands silicon chips and motherboards? Who can read flowcharts? Who determines whether a particular problem is in the software, the hardware, or the operator? Who understands the effect of ultraviolet light on an EPROM? Or what buffers do?

Computer technicians know. And they will be in increasing demand

COURTESY RADIO SHACK, A DIVISION OF TANDY CORPORATION

A technician uses an oscilloscope to trace a malfunction.

as business computers, home computers, instructional computers, and other specialized computers not only grow but skyrocket in use in the United States and around the world.

Computer technicians not only understand *why* a computer performs its speedy and complex functions, they also know the rewards of serving society. They experience a sense of satisfaction when they correct a problem, when they get the ailing computer to perform its wonderful work again. In addition, they will be able to choose from jobs in industry, in private business, or in government. They may also choose to be their own boss.

A Growing Need

Early in the 1980's, about 83,000 people worked as computer service technicians. Most were employed by manufacturers of computer equipment and by companies that provide repair services. Some were employed directly by companies that have large computer systems installed at their own work sites.

Computer technicians most often work in large cities and perform

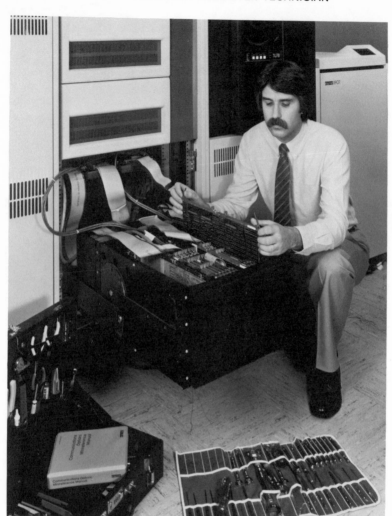

A technician replaces a circuit board in a mainframe computer.

service work for several companies, usually working under a contract arrangement. Job situations vary according to the type of equipment the user has and the technician's special abilities. This type of computer technician must travel from place to place to take care of the computer systems and to make emergency repairs.

Sometimes more than one technician work more or less as a team and service different parts of the same system. Or experienced technicians may work full time at one computer installation and service all phases of one operation.

An important fact is that employment of computer technicians is expected to grow much faster than the average for all occupations through this decade. That means that more jobs will be available for computer technicians than for many other fields. Well-trained computer technicians who are good at their work will be able to choose from many job offers.

As the business climate of the nation expands and becomes healthier, more and more computer equipment will be used and many more technicians will be needed to install and maintain it. Business, government, and other organizations will buy, lease, or rent additional equipment to manage vast amounts of information, control manufacturing processes, and aid in scientific research.

Developing new uses for computers in fields such as education, medicine, traffic control, and agriculture also will create demand for trained technicians.

That strong demand goes hand in hand with the growing number of computers in operation and the locations of those computer installations throughout the nation.

As both the size and the cost of computer hardware become smaller, more and more small companies, organizations, and individuals can afford it. With more computer installations, both the amount of work for the technician and the travel time between locations increase. Each of these factors will increase the number of technicians needed.

Employment of computer service technicians is not likely to be affected by business slumps. Computer operations are rarely cut back or slowed during bad times, so employment for computer service technicians should be steady and secure.

Technicians Are Important to Computer Operation

As we are beginning to see, two basic kinds of workers keep computers computing as their inventors designed them to do. One is the operator. Operators, analysts, and programmers are the users of this sophisticated equipment. They learn how to use it. They give the commands that make it work. They tell it what to do. And the computer does exactly what they tell it to do. If they give correct commands, the computer will operate quickly and efficiently.

A second kind of worker who is important to the operation of a computer is the technician. Computer technicians are very important in a variety of ways.

Some technicians help to build computers, and later other technicians service them.

The builder types of computer technicians, usually called "R and D" or research and development technicians, are very important in the manufacture of new computers. They take the instructions and make the first working model of a new design. They obtain the correct parts and make the connections between those parts. They test and check and recheck as they are building computers or computer elements. They try to prevent breakdowns or problems from occurring. They do their jobs well because computers tend to be very reliable.

However, like anything that is mechanical or made up of interacting parts, computers do sometimes need servicing. That is when speed becomes very important, and the technician must be able to determine —and correct—the problem in the shortest possible time.

Technicians come to the rescue when the computer goes "down," a term meaning that the computer is not performing the functions that operators expect it to do.

In either case, computer technicians must know what and where and when and how and why a computer functions as it does. They must understand much more about how a computer functions than anyone else.

Computer technicians must be able to help the users when there is a problem of any kind. Computer technicians can be like a knight on a white horse, riding to the rescue when someone is in distress.

If you are beginning to think about yourself in that role, and if you are eager to learn, computer technology can carry you into a future that your elders never even dreamed about.

You will be capable, in demand, and confident—even in a rapidly changing future.

Chapter II

Job Prospects

More and more people are recognizing that the computer field offers very real opportunities to those who are willing to invest study and preparation time and to explore new ways to accomplish things.

For instance, let's look first at the booming personal computer market. Retail sales are expected to quadruple from 1982 to 1987. Significant growth will be in large and small corporations, together totaling nearly three-quarters of the market. That gives an indication of the value and expected future impact of personal computers in the business world. Management uses of microcomputers are seen as a strong influencing factor.

Computers for home and educational uses are also growing. Home computers alone are expected to create a market as large as the entire personal computer market during the explosive 1982 growth period.

It is interesting to note that much of the growth in professional use reflects managers and chief executive officers of companies becoming accustomed to having their own desktop computers. The prime difference between managers' computers and clerical-use computers is in the software. Electronic spreadsheets are used increasingly by managers in decision-making. Spreadsheets are software applications that make it possible to process hundreds of numbers at once. With them, managers can find patterns, reach conclusions, and explore alternative courses of action.

Multi-user systems with separate terminals linked to one central unit are losing favor in the market, even though they are a healthy business. But the single-user, or personal, computer that stands alone is rapidly moving out in front. Vendors of these units say that it is more cost-effective for managers to have their own unit. They seem to be proving that point.

In another study by the Department of Commerce, new and unfilled orders for communications equipment are showing a steady stair-step increase, rising to approximately $47 billion by 1984. New orders add up to $15 billion.

These broad looks at the booming computer industry give you some perspective on the projected needs for computer workers.

Let's look at the job outlook for computer technicians in particular.

Employment of computer technicians is expected to grow much faster than the average for all occupations through the 1980's. As the nation's economy expands, more computer equipment will be used and many more technicians will be needed to install and maintain it.

Business, government, and other organizations will buy, lease, or rent additional equipment to manage vast amounts of information, control manufacturing processes, and aid in scientific research. The development of new uses for computers in fields such as education, medicine, and traffic control will also spur demand.

This very strong demand for computer technicians is related to the growing number of computers in operation and their geographic distribution.

Continued reductions in the size and cost of computer hardware will bring the computer within reach of a rapidly increasing number of small organizations. As more and more of these small systems are installed, the amount of time technicians must spend traveling between clients will increase, as will the necessity to service more computer systems.

Employment of computer service technicians is much less likely to be affected by downturns in business activity than is the case in other fields. Because computer operations are not likely to be curtailed during economic slumps, employment of computer service technicians should remain relatively stable.

Let's look at some numbers and percentages.

While jobs in general are expected to increase 17 percent to 25 percent over the next decade, jobs for computer operators will increase by 22 to 30 percent. For computer programmers, opportunities are expected to be up 49 to 60 percent.

As attractive as those figures sound, the prospects for computer service technicians are even better. The job increase in this field will climb a whopping 93 to 113 percent. That means that for every computer technician now working, there will be a need for two technicians by 1990.

This is the highest predicted increase in any work field for the coming decade, according to projections of the United States Department of Labor. One private survey estimated the increase as high as 164 percent.

So we see employment of computer service technicians projected to rise much faster than the average for all occupations through the 1980's as the number of computers in operation continues to increase.

In addition to job openings created by rapid growth, many others will also open up. Replacing workers who transfer, advance in their jobs, or retire will account for more jobs.

If those expectations are not enough, the Department of Labor also sees the youth labor force, ages 16 to 24, declining by about two million young workers. The decline will make it easier to compete for entry-level jobs in all fields.

Computer service technicians tend to be young. About six of every ten openings at the start of this decade were filled by workers in their 20's, many of whom had worked previously in another occupation. As we shall see, occupations that require a knowledge of electronics and provide a good background include business machine repairer, television service technician, and engineering technician.

A significant number of openings were filled by recent graduates of electronics training programs offered by two-year community colleges, trade schools, or vocational schools. Some entered from the military, where they had received both electronics training and work experience.

Translated into specific numbers, the 1980 employment figure of 83,000 is expected to climb to 176,000 by 1990. Each year of this decade, the average number of openings should reach 21,000. This represents 9,000 new jobs and 12,000 replacement jobs.

What does all this mean to you?

Well, it means that if you are interested in a computer technician career, there should be some outstanding opportunities for you.

Not only will there be great numbers of computer service technician jobs open to you, there will also be a great variety of jobs open both in the service field and in industry.

Let's consider some of the possibilities.

Just as a television set is only the means by which entertainment is transmitted into your home, a computer is only a means by which many purposes can be accomplished. The variety of those purposes gives us some idea of how many fields are open to job seekers. It gives us an idea of how a computer technician can become involved in some of the most interesting business fields in the world today. It also gives us some idea of how valuable computer technologists will be as society enters the Information Age.

Let's look at some of the broad uses of computer technology in our society.

A medical specialty known as tomography combines both com-

COURTESY DeVRY INSTITUTE OF TECHNOLOGY

A student faces a diagnostic problem in a camera.

puters and X-ray machines. The X-ray pictures are processed by the computer and produce images of the internal body organs. Analyzing physical problems in this way reduces the need for diagnostic surgery and helps to make sure that operations on the patient are successful.

Computers are important in education. In colleges and schools, students are learning foreign languages, grammar and punctuation, auto mechanics, mathematical and scientific experiments, statistics gathering, and word processing on computers. They can study instructor-prepared materials and learn instantly whether their answers are right or wrong. By using computers, instructors can give each student individualized attention.

Computer-aided instruction (CAI) is making a strong entry into industry as well. For instance, CAI is emerging as a strong contender for improving CAD/CAM (computer-aided design/computer-aided manufacturing) training. Major reasons why business leaders are finding CAI productive include maintaining operator attention, providing a self-paced customized method of instruction, allowing analysis and improvement of weak areas, allowing learners to move at their own pace, providing direct interaction with the ability to answer questions out of sequence, and providing uniformly high-quality instruction. CAI is estimated to reduce learning time by 30 percent. Industry studies show that in 1985 a 30 percent cut in initial operator training time could save $176 million in operator salaries.

Virtually all large manufacturers, department stores, buying services, and sales forces of every description are already moving into automated or computerized warehousing of their products. Efficiency and cost factors in this day and age give them no choice.

Manufacturers are focusing considerable attention on the issue of manufacturing education and its role in reversing current trends in U.S. productivity as compared to other major nations. For all of the twentieth century, the United States has produced more goods per person than any other major nation. Projections now show that France, Germany, and Japan are expected to catch up in the late 1980's. U.S. manufacturers, in order to retain the lead to which the country has been accustomed, are using high technology both in production and in the education that is needed to support manufacturing.

Machine shops control production of machined parts and tools by computer. Increasing amounts of scientific research, which could not have been accomplished by manual or older machine methods, is now done with computers.

Business and service managers use computers to train sales people, service personnel, administrators, nurses, medical technicians, pilots, and many other professionals. Why do they do so? Well, computer training is friendlier and more personal. With it, the trainer can simulate real-life situations. It is proving to be a good way to motivate workers, and with microcomputers such as the Apple or IBM becoming standard in offices, managers are able to create their own instructional and motivational programs.

Other business-office uses of computer systems include budgeting, tracking students, planning, analyzing training needs, evaluating decisions, information processing, text editing, forecasting business trends, analyzing information, keeping records, accounting, and bookkeeping.

Complicated sales forms such as automobile purchase contracts can be computed readily by specially programmed software. Tax accountants rely on computer systems to prepare vast amounts of information, including personal income tax returns for clients.

Even cardiopulmonary resuscitation (CPR) techniques can be taught in less than half an hour using microcomputers. Otherwise, it takes four or more hours. The American Heart Association teaches the technique with an electronic patient, a videotaped demonstration, and an Apple II system that can control the exchange of student and patient responses.

In hospitals, computerized equipment monitors patients during surgery and in all life-threatening situations. Other uses include testing procedures, billing, and record-keeping.

In thousands of offices, multiple copies of letters may now be reproduced automatically through the use of word processing equipment. The letters may be personalized for each recipient, both in the address and in the body of the letter. They may be instantly analyzed for correct spelling. Word processing is also used for editing and for writing books such as this one.

Handicapped persons who have hearing or vision problems are already being helped by speech recognition applications of the computer. Computers can make natural-sounding speech and can pick out spoken words from other sounds. Small words and pictures can be instantly blown up very large on a computer screen for those who have difficulty seeing.

If you are making an airline reservation or buying a ticket to a ballgame, a rock concert, or an opera, computer systems make it possible to get the seat of your choice in a matter of minutes, no matter where you are at the moment of purchase. Similar point-of-sale computer terminals are routinely used in department stores and supermarkets. They not only calculate the cost to you but also make note of inventory information and other records and figure your change.

At the bank teller's station, the current balance in a depositor's account can be immediately available. The same is true for credit ratings of potential customers. All major banking firms process checks and other data by computer. Investment services monitor the stock market and analyze monetary information on desktop computers.

Votes in elections are counted by computers.

Computers can make blurry pictures clear enough to be recognizable. Examples of this use include photographs taken in space and satellite resource photos.

Electrical power systems now rely on computers for planning, design, control, and operation.

Engineers and technology workers use computer programs as they design products, perform drafting functions, and operate machine tools.

Collecting and analyzing drilling data on some of the world's largest oil rigs in the Gulf of Mexico is another significant computer use. That is a 24-hour-a-day, 7-day-a-week activity.

Industrial robots now handle many repetitive or dangerous tasks called for in mass production. Indeed, robotics is a particularly fast-growing segment of high-tech industries. Technicians interested in the field should find interesting opportunities.

Computers can control an entire paper mill, glass factory, or chemical industry. With these processes continuously monitored and regulated by computer, more and better products can be produced efficiently. To give you an idea, computers in the steel industry control rolling mill drive motors of up to 20,000 horsepower.

Performing plant growth experiments on the space shuttle is a function of the first personal computer in space, the Apple II Plus.

Government agencies are beginning to use computerization to save both dollars and energy. Computerization of traffic control in San Jose, California, and water-volume monitoring at the Oroville Dam in northern California are just two of the cost-effective uses.

So far, we've only been talking about business uses of computers.

You may even have a personal computer in your home. Many people do. These microcomputers are bringing their power into the home to be used for games and more and more to perform household services. They will be used to control temperature, provide security, keep records of family money management and maintenance of property, write checks, run slide shows, and organize recipes, just to name a few possibilities. They may also, by using a modem and telephone lines, be connected with larger stores of information including news reports, stock market information, available jobs, dating services, research projects, and more.

Storing and retrieving large amounts of information are among the most important uses of computers, which are, after all, extensions of human brainpower. This function is used extensively by researchers in many labs. It is used by writers, by government, by law enforcement agencies, by public safety workers, and by corporation managers.

Computers are used for traffic control in the air, on the land, and at sea.

They are used in agriculture to schedule planting and harvesting operations, to monitor soils and water content and fertilization.

Are you beginning to see how many uses and how many fields of work are opening up through increasing use of computers?

Technology has changed society before, and now it is changing it again. It is revolutionizing business. In the 1800's the invention and emerging use of industrial machines such as power looms and steam engines radically altered society. Furniture, textile, shoe, firearm, and machine tool factories and railroads transformed life as it was then known. Workers in great numbers no longer worked at their crafts in

Replacing a bad printed-circuit board is easy once the technician has located the malfunction.

individual environments. Economics brought them to the factory and its central power source. Early in this century, the automobile and the airplane radically changed the way we live.

Now the computer is shaping the way we learn and carry on the complex jobs of modern life. Not only is the computer organizing our lives and our businesses, it is also enabling us to produce more goods more economically. Information is becoming the source of power.

Time-shared computer systems and remote terminals as well as microcomputers allow many people to work together from diverse locations. They may work in separate offices, at home, or wherever there is a telephone to link them to the system.

Much of that is possible because workers are doing bigger and bigger jobs with smaller and smaller computers. Tiny silicon chips, known as microprocessors, now do the work that a few years ago was done by room-size machines. As an example, think of the adding machine that your parents or grandparents used and compare it to the credit-card-sized calculators now used to work with numbers.

In short, computers are making possible so many wonderful things that society is beginning to be very dependent upon them.

What does this mean for computer service technicians?

It means that many technicians will be needed to build, install, and service all those computers. Many large installations will be emerging that require full-time on-site maintenance technicians. Remember that the U.S. Department of Labor is projecting an increase of from 93 percent to 113 percent for these jobs in the next ten years? Now do you see why?

With all those computers transforming society, many specialized uses are emerging. Many people will be using them who are computer-literate—they will know how to operate their computer to do the functions they need—but they will depend on computer technology teams (engineers, designers, and technicians) to build the equipment and to service it when something goes wrong. The more important the work they are doing, the more they will need equipment that is always up and ready to respond when they need it.

Chapter **III**

What Does a Computer Technician Do?

Realities of the Job

Technicians who work with computers may be called by a number of titles: computer technician, computer systems service technician, customer engineer, field engineer, customer engineering specialist, customer service trainee, customer service representative, customer service engineer, computer maintenance representative, R & D (research and development) technician, computer electronics technician, computer specialist, microelectronics technician, computer repairer, computer installer, research technician, electronics trouble-shooter, electronics components reliability technician, digital electronics technician, technical associate, calibration technician, lab technician, research associate, or technical sales representative.

Computer service technicians maintain computer systems in top operating condition.

In order to do this, they must be totally familiar with all the equipment they service. In addition to the computer itself, that may include additional (peripheral) equipment such as terminals or monitors, printers, disk drives, card readers, and additional hardware or software.

Technicians usually specialize in a particular computer system or type of repair. Master specialists may be stationed by computer companies in key geographic locations, to be called to solve major repair problems and to provide expertise and assistance to local technicians.

Preventive maintenance, performed according to the manufacturer's recommended schedule, is the primary function of technicians. To do this, the computer system is taken out of operation for a brief time so that its various elements may be checked, cleaned, oiled, or replaced as necessary. Running programs that force the system to operate at the limit of its capabilities enables technicians to discover weaknesses. Locating potential trouble spots in that way allows them to be corrected before they cause the system to break down during normal operation, perhaps at a crucial time.

Other preventive measures that technicians routinely do are cleaning relays, vacuuming, and dusting. Many computers are located in environmentally controlled areas to reduce problems associated with humidity, dust, dirt, smoke, fumes, temperature extremes, or fan breakdowns, any of which can damage delicate computer components. To minimize problems, such work areas also have filtered air, positive force ventilation, and sticky mats at the entrances that pull dust off workers' shoes. Workers often wear white lab coats.

Safety measures to prevent any loss of data also include equipment to monitor power lines. These power surge monitors prevent crashes or loss of computer data in the event of brownouts or power surges. Batteries or generators should be in place for all large installations so that in the event of a power failure, there would be an extra five or ten minutes of back-up power to enable the operator to save the processes in operation at the time. Such a noninterruptible power supply allows the computer operation to be brought to a safe conclusion without loss of data.

While the reliability factor for computers is extremely high and preventive and diagnostic maintenance makes computers even more goof-proof, computer breakdowns still occur. Technicians must correct them and correct them quickly.

These problems require the ability to analyze the system logically. That means that the technician determines where the failure is and what needs to be done to correct it, and then repairs or rectifies the problem. Troubleshooting is another word to describe the process, which essentially is a process of elimination and deduction.

One of the technician's first steps is to determine whether there are operator problems, often called "cockpit" problems. Although manufacturers take great pains to build computers that are user-friendly, idiot-proof, or otherwise easy to use, there is always the possibility that an untrained operator or one unfamiliar with a particular process may hit the wrong keys and jam a computer. Another term for this is locking up the system. The computer, after receiving an unusual command that conflicts with its programmed expectations, may simply stop everything. The operator may think the system has broken down. The technician needs to know how to differentiate between a locked up computer caused by an operator and an equipment failure.

Many computers now have built-in automatic diagnostic routines

COURTESY APPLE COMPUTER CO.

A technician troubleshoots a prototype as a supervisor gives assistance.

that tell the operator what the problem is in the event of failure. Other diagnostic routines may be part of the technician's responsibility. Once the source of the failure is determined, the technician frequently replaces a card or memory board. He may replace a module, which is a subassembly of up to four or five boards. Often these working boards or modules are simply sent back to the manufacturer for repair or are considered "B E R" (beyond economical repair). When repair costs are very high, time literally becomes money. It is cheaper to replace a working board with a new one than it would be to repair it.

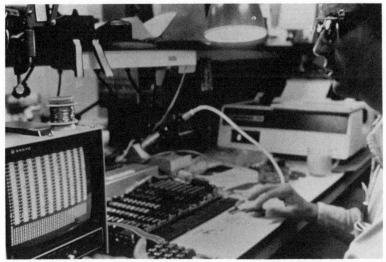

COURTESY APPLE COMPUTER CO.

A bench technician uses a monitor for test purposes.

Troubleshooting can be an extremely complicated process because of the complexity of the many computer systems. For instance, the system may have interconnected parts or components that were manufactured by different companies. Terminals for data entry and retrieval may be located in work areas separated by considerable distances. Other systems may have been designed to run many programs at once.

The installation of new computer systems is another job that computer technicians perform. Technicians prepare them for use, to sell supplies, keep maintenance records for each installation serviced, and recommend operating procedures to new computer users to help to keep repairs at a minimum.

Continuing self-education is a basic part of a computer technician's job. It includes studying new models of computers and related equipment, reading technical journals and manuals, and attending company-sponsored training sessions.

Third-party Maintenance

Servicing computers is rapidly becoming a separate and significant business.

Think about this.

Suppose you owned or operated one (or more!) of these amazing machines and then one day, right in the middle of the most important accounting studies or information-gathering reports you've ever done, right when you're counting on meeting a crucial deadline, right when you've worked for days or weeks or hours getting everything just so, the display information locks up or says "Error!" or the copy won't print or whatever.

How would you feel? What would you do? You certainly wouldn't kick or pound your machine—it might just swallow all that wonderful work.

And, though your computer has never done this before and you have always been happy with it and you think the manufacturer is the best in the business, you may not want to call the manufacturer for help because company headquarters is six or ten states away. Who could expect them to make house calls at that distance?

You probably wouldn't want to cry either, because any type of liquid dripping on a computer really damages the equipment.

If it's not brand-new or still under warranty, the dealer may—or may not—be able to help. Usually, if it is a microcomputer, he would ask you to bring it in.

You might scream or moan. That might make you feel better—but it wouldn't solve the problem.

Can you visualize the scene? Can you feel the sense of panic? of helplessness?

That is the moment that needs, absolutely needs, a good computer technician. Someone who KNOWS what to do. Someone who can get your problem solved immediately—if not sooner. Someone who is like a Boy Scout or Girl Scout—dependable, trustworthy, loyal, friendly— you've got the picture.

And if you can see the hero qualities, the possibility of pursuing rewarding work, the satisfaction of achieving worthwhile daily results, you may be thinking that you really want to be a technician. And not just any old technician, but a good technician. A *very* good technician.

A frustrated customer doesn't want someone to scream with, or the wrong expert who only knows some other piece of equipment. A frustrated computer user wants someone who is cool, calm, and collected. Someone who will make the world of information run smoothly again. Soneone who will do it in the shortest possible time. When modern people get used to miracles, they want them to continue. They don't want to remember yesterday; they want to continue today's work on schedule. Time is money, and they feel they can't afford to waste it.

Good Technicians Needed

Joe works for TRW in the Service Management program. Like his 2,800 co-workers, he has been well trained and he is ready for this type of emergency call.

He works out of Los Angeles, California, but his colleagues may be headquartered in Fairfield, New Jersey, or Dallas, Texas, or any one of 200 other locations nationwide.

Joe knows that proper service requires proper coverage. He knows that he or one of the others has to be where the customer is and that he has to respond to the customer when and where there is a need. He knows that he must be fast.

Another thing Joe knows is that any computer or related product is only as good as the service that supports it—throughout its useful life. He feels good about the fact that his employer only agrees to service quality products. That means that there is an immediate good chance that the problem is solvable.

Before Joe started working as a computer service technician, he was a math major, a computer buff, and graduated from a two-year electronic technology program at his local community college. When he started with TRW, he was given classroom training from A to Z in theory and in practice and hands-on laboratory training on all kinds of equipment—just like the machines he is now called on to repair for customers. His was take-it-apart-and-put-it-back-together-again training.

Even though Joe has been repairing computers and peripherals for almost seven years, his training has never ceased. An endless flow of new and updated service publications and local and regional seminars keeps him up-to-date. He knows that it is this kind of training and education that ensures his knowing what to look for and how to correct problems fast. It helps him to take pride in his work to know that his supervisors and managers share his dedication and his desire to be prepared to solve any problem.

Another thing that makes Joe feel comfortable is knowing that TRW's computer communications network links its entire national field with its New Jersey headquarters. With that kind of control of its gigantic spare parts and printed-circuit board inventory, Joe knows that he can get the proper parts to repair equipment with a minimum of downtime. As a matter of fact, this computerized parts inventory tracking system is so complete that it even covers the individual repair kits in any of 2,000 field representatives' cars. That makes it possible to obtain emergency parts from the nearest possible location. This parts tracking system has helped Joe on more than one weekend emergency.

Every delay that can be shortened means more savings of both time and money for the customer.

Sam works for the same company, but he's a bench technician. He's trained up to the microprocessor chip level, which includes repairing circuit boards and mechanical assemblies.

Repair facilities in each location are able to ensure reusable spares. Last year, nationwide, they repaired some 300,000 printed-circuit boards for more than 80,000 end users. And each time they repaired one, they brought it up to the manufacturer's latest specifications and modifications, so that each one serviced was automatically updated.

Joe and the other service representatives know just how long any repair job should take. If he has any problem completing it in the expected time, he notifies his manager and back-up assistance is available. This type of early warning alert system is all part of the number one goal—SERVICE—that Joe and others like him are seeking to provide.

Working in this type of service management company gives Joe some company benefits that he finds helpful in doing his job.

For instance, TRW's continuation engineering program provides recommendations for product modifications that cut down on service time and increase the reliability of the equipment. Its performance reporting system provides the manufacturing company's engineers with machine failure information. While the manufacturing of computers is a very competitive industry, a separate service management organization can work hand-in-hand with individual manufacturers to continually upgrade products. Technicians' keen observation of malfunctions and suggestions for improvement can result in product improvements. When they detect a frequently occurring problem, for instance, they can report both the problem and a possible solution.

Company policy also gives Joe the freedom to recommend new equipment, upgrades, and peripherals to customers when it would be to their advantage. In fact, it encourages him to do so.

Maynard D. Smith, vice president and general manager of TRW's Customer Service Division, gives his viewpoint: "The very nature of the service business tends to bring the field technician to the realization that he or she is working directly for the customer. This is a business concept we tend to nurture and expand, because our business is only as good as our response time." Recommending product enhancements that increase reliability and reduce maintenance time is seen in the same light. Service is what they are selling. It's as if the field representatives were part of the customer's personal service staff and the products utilized were part of the customer's inventory.

Joe has another company back-up service to depend on. He can call in to TRW's technical support group, a fully computerized polling center that allows him to have very sophisticated diagnostic information always available. This ability to troubleshoot over the phone also helps Joe in getting down equipment up and running again in a minimum amount of time.

In both telephone troubleshooting and diagnosing problems of equipment that operates with the use of phone lines, technical personnel in the polling center play a key role in determining whether there is something wrong with the computer system or with the telephone lines. That is a particularly vexing problem, and technicians on duty must have credibility with the phone company. That credibility hinges on their training, experience, and ongoing interaction with the phone company.

It may sound as if Joe were cutting his own salary by being so efficient and working so quickly. Nothing could be further from the truth. The happier his customers are, the more they trust him and turn to him again. The more they recommend him to others, the more business grows for Joe's company. Joe's reputation as well as that of his employer is always based on how good a job he did the last time the customer needed him. It's as simple—and as important—as that.

Joe not only feels good about himself and the job he is doing, but he also tends to have variety because he is in touch with a variety of people each day. Making them happy tends to make Joe's day better. And who doesn't want to have a good day?

Customer Service

Preventive maintenance and servicing of equipment are a cost of doing business. Both are necessities in the world of high technology.

Interestingly, however, trends and changes appear imminent. The traditional image of repair personnel carrying heavy tool kits appears to have a limited future in the Information Age.

More and more, the computer service technician will be a white-collar worker and will possess a higher level of intellectual skills. The technician of the future will be involved in lifelong learning because keeping pace with rapidly changing technology will require it.

Instructing customers in routine preventive care will also be an increasing part of the service. The demand will be so great that even talking and teaching their way out of some future service calls will not diminish the service work load.

Instilling confidence and feelings of security will be integral to the job as customers become more and more dependent on the new technology. The service technician will not only be bringing technical expertise to the machines and workers who depend on him or her to do so, but will also be a visible human element in a technological world. Troubleshooting and problem-solving give evidence that human brainpower is in communication with the computers and available to the customer.

A multipurpose technician who can "fix anything" may not be on the scene. Increasingly, technicians will specialize in particular equipment. Some will be field service technicians or representatives. Others will be bench- or component-level repair technicians. Some will travel to the customer's computer location; others will remain in a depot repair center. Some will be available for troubleshooting over the phone.

Some computer service technicians will be employed by the manufacturer's service agency, some by independent computer dealers, and many by third-party maintenance firms.

Industry Service Careers

Let's take a closer look at the service careers that are a direct segment of the manufacturing industry.

Radio Shack, a division of Tandy, is a good example. This company operates 292 computer repair facilities at locations across the United States.

IBM is known for its own follow-up service and the service orientation of its entire operation. Others of the largest manufacturers that provide their own service bureaus include Digital Equipment, Texas Instruments, Wang, and Lanier.

Entry-level Opportunities

What can a beginning technician expect in a first job?

With minimum background—high school diploma, an aptitude for mathematics, electronics theory instruction, and supervised practice in electronics—you should be able to land an entry-level job with a computer repair firm at an annual starting salary of $13,000 to $15,000.

If you have an associate in science degree in electronic engineering or technology from a good community college, college, or vocational school, your starting salary is more likely to be $16,000 to $19,000.

Often new repair technicians start out in field service. Servicing microcomputers is considerably different from working on minicomputers and mainframes. Because sophisticated diagnostic devices are not as likely to be built into personal computers yet, microcomputer field service is usually limited to replacement of printed-circuit boards and other gross modules of a system, which is a comparatively simple operation. This type of repair service at the customer's premises may be a good starting position for new technicians.

Bench Work

More advanced (and higher-paying) work involves troubleshooting and repairing on a component level. One example might be isolating and replacing a defective memory chip so that an entire module becomes usable again.

This bench-test repair is usually done at a depot repair center. Depending on experience, component-level repair technicians can earn $19,000 to $25,000 or more.

Local Opportunities

Many independent computer dealers as well as computer franchises provide their own repair facilities with support from the computer and peripheral manufacturers.

Pay scales at individual stores tend to be lower than at the larger service operations and large manufacturers, but job requirements for beginning workers may be a little more flexible. There may even be opportunity for part-time work while you are completing your education.

Tom, like many computer technicians now servicing franchised retail computer stores, has taken advantage of numerous and varied training opportunities to arrive at a job that he finds very rewarding. His electronics interests started with a data processing class in the first year of college. He then enlisted in the Air Force, choosing the "longest course" in communication and relay computer equipment followed by working with tele-autograph machines and cryptographic equipment. His next job was with IBM, servicing memory typewriters and office copiers. His desire to pursue ownership of his own business took him out of electronics for a few years before an unusual twist of fate brought him to an auto manufacturing plant where he was, after a plant retrenchment, eligible for a company-sponsored retraining program. Again, Tom chose computers, including advanced digital electronics.

By this time, Tom had built his own unique background from several types of electronics training and experience. He also had a record of at least two years in each of these positions.

Now he is the technician at one of the more than 200 Computerland stores and finds the work challenging and interesting. He likes the hands-on experience with new machines. "Here," he says, "I have to be a real people person. There is a lot of pressure; people are irate or frustrated if their equipment doesn't work, and they need to talk to someone they feel they can trust." Not everyone trained to be a technician can be an effective repairman, he feels, and the ability to relate well with people is the necessary quality to be successful.

Tom is visibly interested in his work, another quality that he feels is significant. "You have to be super curious," he says. "There is so much to learn. Things are changing so fast, and every new machine is like meeting a new person." He dedicates time every night to read for at least an hour to keep pace with the industry, although he points out that "nobody can keep up with it all." He uses the word "curiosity" often in relation to his work and applies it to peripherals as well as the basic hardware. Every part of the system, as well as the user, is interrelated. He says that technicians must understand cause and effect in order to pinpoint the problem.

Tracing the malfunction to a particular module or chip accounts for much of Tom's repair servicing. At that point, he generally swaps rather than fixes the inoperative part. One reason is that if ten or more functions are imbedded in a single chip, there is no way to separate the functions.

Most of the machines Tom services are carried into the store because it is easier and cheaper. But he does travel to users' locations when necessary.

He sees a growing future and looks toward combining repair and sales for the greatest personal financial rewards.

Independent Technicians

Some technicians choose to operate their own repair facility, either as a total career or as a second, moonlighting option.

For example, Allan chose a disk-drive service as his second career. He has been into electronics in one way or another since he was thirteen. He has sold parts in retail electronics stores, worked in the electronics industry, and is currently an engineering technologist specializing in advanced digital equipment, microprocessors, and designing of new data cartridges with a research department of a major corporation.

Allan chose disk drives as his service specialty because, to most people, "they are a mechanical nightmare." Disk drives are the most likely part of a computer system to develop problems and often the most difficult to pinpoint and correct. His equipment includes a stand-alone drive exerciser, with which the disk drive operates independent of the computer, and also specialized software for checking errors. The biggest problems that send his customers seeking help are read problems (the information is not being read and used correctly), misalignment, or dirty heads. While he finds the actual work challenging and interesting, he must also utilize advertising efficiently in order to build up a clientele and get enough work. He believes that manufacturers try to discourage the small independent repair service. He also sees a limited life expectancy for his type of repair service, perhaps five years or so, because of the coming of bubble memory on a chip that will do away with the need for floppy disk drives.

But Allan is versatile. He continues to grow and change with the industry, expecting to continue with whatever new changes and products come into acceptance.

Other Technicians in Industry

While computer service technicians or computer repair technicians may be most easily identified, there are tremendous opportunities for other types of skilled computer technicians in industry. Opportunities are expanding in direct relation to the growth of computers in our society. Some relate to the uses of the computer itself as the most modern, efficient way to get a job done. Others pertain to the continual upgrading of the computer and the computer's ability to perform better and faster.

Using the Newest Tools Available

Industry has very real needs for people who are experts in specific fields. Some of those needs are for electronic design engineers, solid state and optical physicists, material scientists, chemists, and computer scientists (hardware and software). Each of these fields also needs technician support. Basically, technicians put theory into practice.

Computers have become commonplace in all of these job fields, and major corporations such as Honeywell want men and women who can not only offer expertise in a particular science but also do their work on the newest tools available: computers.

CAD/CAM is a key phrase in this technology. It is an acronym for

Computer *A*ided *D*esign and *C*omputer *A*ided *M*anufacture. CAD/ CAM is becoming increasingly important to American industry.

CAD figures heavily in the design of integrated circuit chips, for instance. It is increasingly an integral part of drafting. CAD helps companies, both large and small, to make more complete use of their highly experienced people.

CAM describes the use of the computer in manufacturing for such functions as handling of inventory, efficient parts distribution, assembly and shipping functions, or sending parts straight from the design department to the manufacturing area.

In many of these areas, electronics technicians have been a major part of the working team. They have been updating their skills to include computer expertise as industry changes.

Other business functions such as banking and insurance have relied on large numbers of clerical, semiskilled, or unskilled workers. With the aid of computers, they have been and will be increasingly moving in the direction of specialized technical operators.

New technician jobs in these areas are opening up daily. Each new application of high technology seems to snowball, opening up further possibilities and jobs. These are not merely jobs for technicians doing work similar to that of other technicians; they are specialized new tasks and applications within a growing field.

Networking and telecommunications are good examples.

For years, society has depended on telephones for oral communication and on postal delivery for the transmittal of written letters and documents.

The advent of networks and telecommunications, linking computers and computer output over hundreds or thousands of miles, is opening the door to almost-instant communication of complex and important information. Electronic mail is a term used to describe this rapidly growing technology. Technicians are vital to the installation, implementation, and use of electronic mail.

Modems, or data sets, are specific and separate electronic devices that perform modulation and demodulation functions that permit the rapid communication of information over telephone circuits. The information can go directly into the computer's memory or into the storage files.

Research and Development Technicians

Technicians are heavily involved in research and development as support personnel for engineers, designers, and scientists. Technicians have a particular responsibility for making new ideas work, for translating new theories into workable realities. Technicians tend to be practical. They are realists. Working with their hands and making things function makes them valuable to producers of new products.

Technicians working directly with engineers often use their ideas and carry out the engineer's technical plan. Technicians are the doers rather than the initiators, although they may also design or make improvements.

Technicians are important practical persons with a sound knowledge of scientific principles. They must know testing and measuring devices as well as practical electrical and mechanical techniques.

An engineering technologist is also a practical person who applies engineering principles and organizes and oversees production, construction, or operation. The technologist generally has extended the associate degree to a four-year bachelor's degree. In industry, technicians and technologists are part of the engineering team. They accomplish practical objectives by applying proven techniques, methods, and procedures. They are specialists in methodology, and their manual skills are responsible for developing the concepts and plans of engineers.

Technicians, after receiving instruction, may develop breadboards, make prototypes, or build the first working model of a new design. They are responsible for getting the correct parts, making connections, wire-wrapping, and many other intricate functions that are integral to the project.

So great is the need for electronic technicians with knowledge of computers that occupational training conversion programs are being set up for civil service employees to retrain workers whose previous job functions have become obsolete.

One such program, known as PLATO (Programmed Learning for Automatic Teaching Operations), was given at Pt. Mugu, California. Twenty-three selected upward mobility students underwent an intensive nine-month, full-time classroom program. At its conclusion, all were placed in technician positions at a GS-5 level. Advancement should take them to a GS-9 level.

ATE, or *A*utomated *T*est *E*valuation, is another field to note carefully. Technicians specializing in this field use increasingly sophisticated automatic equipment to test assembled or loaded printed-circuit boards for failed components or incorrect component values. They may also test the integrity of the printed-circuit board itself.

Automatic test equipment is very complex, very large. Each printed-circuit board (board A, board B, etc.) to be tested has its own bed-of-nails test fixture. The ATE monitor takes readings at precise test points and lists errors on a printed strip of paper, which then goes with the printed-circuit board to the repair technician.

Use of automated test equipment saves hours of tedious technician test analysis. It is also creating a new specialty in the field of technology.

Security

Technicians working within the computer industry will find security increasingly tight. Technology wars are not just talk. Business stakes are high as every effort is made to prevent technological secrets from being smuggled from one company to another, from one country to another. Company loyalty becomes a valued trait for employees at all levels. That's part of the good salary, part of the business relationship.

High-technology companies frequently offer stock option plans to employees. This is more than just monetary reward. It allows the employee to have a direct financial stake in the success of the company. It increases company loyalty.

Jack's career in industry illustrates some of these points. He first studied petroleum engineering. When he found that it wasn't a good choice for him, he enlisted in the Air Force. There he went to electronics school and did superior work. Sticking with it was an easy choice. Upon his discharge, he completed an associate in science degree in electronics at a community college. While in school, he worked part time in radio-TV repair.

After graduation, he worked first in guided missiles and related aerospace technology. Ultimately, he moved into medical electronics with a second major corporation. As high tech came into its own, he began to need computer technology as well as broad-base electronics. Growing with the industry has been a part of his career. He is now a supervisor.

Keeping up is a definite part of his career. He reads a great deal and also builds and experiments with electronics outside of working hours. He has been in the business twenty-nine years and still enjoys his work.

Chapter IV

Are You a Good Candidate?

Questions, questions, questions. The world is full of them. Selecting a few to ask yourself—and then pursuing the answers—will help you to determine whether a computer technician career is for you.

Do you have a keen interest in computers?

Do you have an insatiable curiosity about computers and computer uses?

If your answers to those two questions are a strong yes, you have a good indication that you should seriously consider a computer career. Motivation plays a strong role in achieving success. There is no substitute for choosing to concentrate on something that interests you strongly. When you like what you are doing, chances are that you will do it well.

How well do you know yourself? Think about that. Success in your work often depends upon more than your personal knowledge of the facts relating to the job. Three factors play important roles in assessing yourself, according to the American Association of Engineering Societies: aptitude, interest, and determination. This book will give you some insights into those areas.

Personal characteristics as well as good oral and written communication skills are necessary because of the continual interaction that technicians have with customers. Technicians must have a businesslike attitude. They must be able to talk to customers and to communicate with people who know both more and less than they do about computers. It is highly important for them to initiate and maintain good relationships with both computer operators and management staffs. Good human relations is often the key to success, and it becomes increasingly important in a world dominated by impersonal machines.

You must be able to reason logically. That means thinking like a computer—in logical, sequential steps. It means using a systematic approach to getting things accomplished.

31

You must have a sense of responsibility. People will be depending on you to see that their computers do exactly what they need exactly when they need it done. Your ability to understand their needs and push yourself to see that they achieve their important purposes is an important part of the job. You must realize that their deadline is your deadline. Excuses do not get the job done, and getting the job done is what you will be required to do, no matter what.

Because technicians normally handle job assignments alone, they must be able to work without close supervision. They must have the initiative to start their work, stick to it, and follow through. They must be capable. They must be able to carry out assignments independently.

Patience is an asset. Computer malfunctions are often difficult to pinpoint. Doing the necessary detective work to discover the cause and the location may take time. It may be painstaking. The ability to stay calm, to wait, to check and recheck requires a nature that is patient.

Leadership skills are also a plus. Climbng career ladders is dependent upon the ability to supervise others and to generate the kind of respect that inspires other less skilled workers.

What is your knowledge level? What level are you willing to attain through work and study? Jobs as computer technicians require specialized knowledge of mathematics, computer equipment, and computer software or applications programs. Some jobs may also require engineering training. Skill levels in these areas become part of your overall assessment and indicate qualities that you would bring to your own job future.

Are you trustworthy? Some employers will require a security check on you because of the confidential nature of the data processed by many of their customers and also because of the competitive nature of the high-technology field.

What is your physical condition? Physical requirements for computer technicians include normal hearing because many problems are diagnosed by slight variations in the sounds the computer system makes. Freedom from color blindness is necessary to ensure that you can make proper connection of color-coded wires.

Technicians must also be able to lift equipment weighing up to 60 pounds. And general good health means that you can be a dependable worker.

What Are Your Expectations?

The business world in general and the world of computers in particular may be pretty much of a mystery to you. Business environments are not exactly like the world of high school or even college. It may be hard to visualize what lies ahead.

The kinds of expectations that you can begin to think about, however, do relate to some things that are already familiar.

If you like to build things or to fix things, you already know some of the inner satisfactions that come with that kind of accomplishment. Does a new and functioning project that came alive as a result of your hands and your brainpower bring a real high? It should!

Does fixing a damaged or malfunctioning object give you a reward that is both internal and external? Identifying a potential source of trouble and heading it off at the pass, so to speak, brings with it a sense of personal value. After all, you are preventing catastrophe and making it possible for yourself or others to achieve positive results and to do the job well.

Do you like to work alone? Technical work is frequently solitary work. There may be others nearby—you wouldn't be a hermit—but liking to figure things out for themselves is a quality that technicians must call upon frequently.

Is problem-solving a real challenge for you? Do you like to analyze something, figure out how it works and how it can work better? Is problem-solving more interesting to you than following a regular routine?

How are you at getting along with others? Do you enjoy doing favors or providing service for someone? Can you request an item or make a purchase politely and intelligently? How are your listening skills? Are you good at understanding directions?

Are you independent? Can you take responsibility and do a job without repeated reminders? Does beginning, doing, and ending a job by yourself give you a sense of satisfaction? A good feeling about yourself in relation to your work can be worth even more to you than the size of your paycheck.

Does it please you to make others happy or satisfied with the results of your work?

Does understanding the mysteries of transistors, resistors, silicon chips, integrated circuits, and other technical parts excite you? Are you hooked on figuring out and knowing what all those little parts do?

Do you like to know and understand things that others do not? Although more and more people are becoming computer-literate to meet job demands or their own interests, most of them will not know very much about the inside workings of a computer. Using a computer is coming to be like driving a car—everyone needs to know how to operate one. But the person who understands *why* computers work their magic and is able to keep computers functioning has a unique role in the future of society. It's a little like knowing a secret, or getting an A in math when your friends are pulling Cs.

Those are among the qualities that could determine your satisfaction in a job as a computer technician. They may be clues to help you discover your future in this career field.

Chapter V

Education and Training

When it comes to getting a head start in a chosen career, computer buffs have a unique and almost unprecedented opportunity to start early.

Children as young as three years of age are getting turned on to computers now. Games make it easy, interesting, and exciting for them.

Young people start by making faces, chasing gum drops, zapping asteroids, waging sea battles, matching alphabet letters, producing kaleidoscopic graphics at the touch of a key, drawing images, making posters, or doing math. Or any of thousands of other possibilities.

It all seems like fun and games, yet even very young children are learning the new technology in a practical, painless, and stimulating way.

By the teen years, an amazing new world is virtually at your fingertips. If the substance of it intrigues you, if the high-tech frontier excites you, you can invest some of your fun and leisure time into activities that will prepare you for a solid career. Remember that one definition of success is finding something that you enjoy doing and learning to do it so well that people will pay you for doing it. That definition is particularly open to wise and alert young people who are transforming their computer game intrigue into a lifetime career goal.

A little planning can start you on the path toward finding big dividends.

Read, read, read is good advice. Introductory computer books, computer magazines, computer business news in your local newspaper, analysis of future trends of the Information Age such as in *Megatrends* by John Naisbitt—all will help you to build your understanding of the industry.

Opportunities for learning through regular classroom instruction, computer camps, short-term fee computer classes for youth offered by community colleges or community service organizations, or special

COURTESY MOUNT SAN ANTONIO COLLEGE

Learning computer fundamentals is integral to being able to service computers.

events presented by local computer dealers are among introductory programs available. Friends may have a home computer and invite you over to see what it can do.

The most valuable learning opportunity, however, is having your own computer to use consistently. You can buy a computer for under $100, perhaps with money you have earned by baby-sitting or yard work, and begin learning to program and to understand how computers work. When it is your computer, you have access to it as often as you like. You will learn not to be afraid of it. You will learn that mistakes can be eliminated, that you can direct it to do some fascinating things, that it will obey you (even if you give it an incorrect command), and that you are capable of making it do things that may bewilder your parents and surprise your friends. Your parents may help you to get your own computer if they know you are serious about learning this new technology. Even if they are somewhat apprehensive about computers, they may realize that your world will be heavily populated with computers and that, for you, computer literacy will be necessary.

A word of warning: You should keep in mind, if you are getting serious about computers, that an inexpensive computer will not be your best investment. You will be disappointed if you expect an inexpensive computer, perhaps one that is primarily meant for games, to do all the functions that a more complex machine can accomplish. You will need one that can handle peripherals (like monitor, disk drives, and printer) and one with a good supply of software available. The computer you choose should also be capable of being updated.

If you are technically minded and like to work with your hands, you can get much more involved if you also choose to experiment with parts and electronic gadgets. You may want to build your own computer in order to learn the inner mysteries of this fascinating box. That may be a thoughtful choice—or it may be prompted by a definite passion to gain electronic knowledge. And there's no telling where that can lead.

By the time Kourosh (Kory) Hamzeh was graduating from Rolling Hills High School, he was launching his own computer company, Euclid Computer, in Torrance, California. Kory became interested in telecommunications when he was twelve. He used junk parts and mail-order components to build his own equipment for tracking satellites. In 1979 he began designing computer systems as his own personal challenge.

Not only has Kory designed an extremely fast, economical, low-priced, industry-respected computer system, but he has eight people working for him. He and his engineer brother, Fariborz (Fari), are ready to bring his computer system to market. Kory insists that he is not a genius or possessed of special talents, but he does acknowledge working harder than others his age. Putting in sixty to seventy hours a week building and perfecting his computer system in addition to his high school studies (he carries a B+ average) brought him to the threshold of industry success while still in his teens. It is also bringing him the chance to work with one of only fifty superchips recently developed by Intel, because that company's sales engineers had been watching Kory's design engineering capabilities and moved to make another significant challenge available to him.

Other teenagers have had varying success stories as a result of their experience with computers. One young man, before his sixteenth birthday, earned $85,000 with programs and manuals that he wrote.

For every celebrity-size early success story, however, there are uncounted similar stories that give teenagers a practical and reachable head start on interesting computer careers. Early skill development and success experiences do allow you to jump into your first full-time job with some solid experience to help you open that door.

Tinkering with transistors and resistors or relay circuitry or other gadgets may prove exciting to you. Learning what effect each has on another, or how to solder, or why an existing switch works may capture your interest. Making something work may ignite a passion that will lead you to discover capabilities you didn't know you possessed.

When the introductory or little things are well mastered, you may want to build your own microcomputer.

How do you get started on such a project? That may turn out easier and more interesting than you first realized.

For instance, choosing a Heathkit microprocessor trainer kit can be both an adventure and an education. The manual that comes with the kit gives you step-by-step directions for building the microprocessor, each with a space to check off as you go.

You will need to learn quickly that computers follow a very logical sequence. There are no short-cuts or steps that can be skipped. Patience in following that sequence and checking for accuracy as you go can save hours and hours of frustration.

Building the Heathkit microprocessor trainer helps you to learn that important lesson as well as the actual components and relationships necessary for a functioning unit.

When you have completed the trainer, you will be able to continue this phase of your self-education with the aid of Heath's cassette directions and a handy flip chart. The flip chart is color-coded, graphically attention-holding, and, together with the cassette directions, leads you step by step through the process of understanding and using what others might consider a complicated piece of equipment.

Although the microprocessor is not, by itself, a computer, you can add other components to get it to microcomputer usage.

Heath also has an H-100 16-bit computer in its line of computer kits; Multitech Electronics has the Micro-Professor teaching device kit; Netronics has the 16-bit Explorer, and there are others. Ads in magazines such as *Radio Electronics* can help you in locating kits, parts, and information. There, too, you will find such things as government-surplus electronic equipment catalogs. You may find this type of discovery somewhat addictive.

Electronic hobbyists often begin with a kit and then progress to building equipment from individual parts and instructions in books, manuals, or magazines. If you know someone who likes to do this, you may be able to persuade him or her to help you, to give you hints, or to let you watch or help when he is working on a project.

As you gain expertise, friends and others may begin turning to you for help. That is what you want to happen. It means that you are beginning to have some mastery in a body of knowledge. The more you have, the more in demand you will be. It can lead you to career opportunities, especially if you find out by experience that you enjoy it.

If you have your own computer, it will prove very beneficial to join a users' club. Some clubs include more than one type of computer, but most are specifically geared to Apple or TRS-80 or IBM or another

COURTESY SAN JOSE CITY COLLEGE

Students use micro trainers in a learning lab setting.

specific computer. In fact, when purchasing a computer, you should always take care to choose one that has ample software and lots of other owners available. Learning together with others will help you immensely. Who would want to have to learn *everything* alone?

Joining a users' club will also give you an opportunity to meet other hobbyists, technicians, and computer enthusiasts. Their discoveries are contagious, and the contacts they provide may lead you exactly where you want to go.

Formal Education

Although your own expertise can pay off for you more readily in the computer field than in other more established fields, it is becoming more and more necessary to have formal education.

For those aiming at computer technician careers, there are a number of choices. Your ultimate career goal will determine how much and what kind of technical education you choose.

Starting in junior high and high school, you should choose as much math and science as you can. You should give your best attention to math and science classes, projects, and homework because the information you learn there will provide a good foundation for your computer technician career. Not only that, but the knowledge gained in those subjects becomes increasingly interesting as it becomes understood. A solid math-science foundation not only is necessary for your entry-level or first job but also provides a base from which you can build as you later move to advance your career.

When you graduate from high school, your choices become a bit more complex. You can choose to work toward a four-year bachelor of science degree in computer sciences or computer technology, or you can plan for a two-year associate in science or associate in arts degree at a community college. Often, with good planning, the two-year degree can be transferred to a four-year college or university, thus completing the first two years at considerably less cost. You may be able to go directly to an entry-level job for which the company will train you and even pay you while you train. Although that is sometimes possible, you should consider that, in the long run, the higher-paying jobs usually go to the people with the sought-after degrees.

It is important to read college catalogs and class schedules to become familiar with the educational programs available. You can visit or write the colleges and request catalogs and schedules. (There may be a small fee for catalogs.) You should also know that titles and programs vary. You may have to ask specific questions of counselors or instructors to learn which classes and programs are the best choice for you. Seek several opinions and weigh them carefully. Do they reinforce other opinions? Do they make sense? Are they clear? Do they match with the career goals you have in mind? Talk to both educators and people employed in industry, if possible. Make the effort to read and compare. It will pay you to do so.

The two-year associate degree in some specialized electrical discipline such as electronics technology, electrical power technology, or computer technology is generally considered the most effective way to become prepared as a technician. Many community colleges also offer shorter certificate courses.

Some companies, however, are beginning to require a four-year technology degree. Often these companies may use the term field engineers to describe their computer technologists. Objectives and features of a four-year technology degree center on use of current application information and practices for specific technical problems, applying technical knowledge and techniques to current technical problems, solving practical design problems, learning evaluation techniques for industrial problems, and developing complex current design procedures in a specialized technical area.

Community colleges are good places to obtain a two-year technology degree. Computer technology programs may include such courses as computer logic, computer sub-systems, computer systems seminar, fundamentals of computer science, or computer programming. Electronics, electronics labs, computer-aided drafting, and several semesters of electronics mathematics are also required. Course names and content vary from college to college. You may also find micro-integrated circuits, storage principles and devices, input/output devices, electromechanical components, industrial safety, computer mathematics, or computer logic and arithmetic. Most of those classes would also transfer to four-year schools if you raise your sights and want to go on to get a bachelor's degree. Be sure that you know which ones transfer before you begin your study.

Many students find it worthwhile to keep all their options open. Obtaining a two-year degree gives them a concrete employable achievement. It is good insurance for the future and looks well on a résumé. At the same time, choosing courses that will transfer can save valuable time if there is any chance at all that you may want to continue working for your four-year degree either immediately as a full-time student or as a part-time student after working hours. Always determine in advance which classes and programs will transfer. The two-year associate degree should enable you to get a good beginning job, and the employer may then be willing to pay for your additional education.

Experience While Learning

While pursuing your computer technology study at a community college, you should be in immediate contact with the college's job placement office. It may be able to direct you to intern jobs in local industry or part-time jobs in labs or offices on the campus. Those will add practicality to your study approach, spending money, and perhaps motivation and contacts as you consider your future.

You may want to consider volunteer jobs as a way to gain experience while you are learning. In addition to considering philanthropic, political, or charitable organizations, which are always looking for volunteers, you should be alert to special opportunities in both the private and the public sectors. For instance, the city of Oxnard in California accepted volunteer computer programming students to work with its newly installed computer system. One of those students also volunteered to help set up equipment in the new computer lab at the local community college. Such invested hours become valuable experience when it comes time to apply for the first full-time job.

An interesting nonprofit, student-run enterprise at Diablo Valley College in California gives students some solid experience while they are learning. Called Diablo Valley Enterprises, Inc., this corporation manufactures MST-80B microcomputer trainers, which are then sold to government agencies, private industry, and other colleges and high schools. The well-planned cooperative understanding, launched by the electronics department of Diablo Valley College in cooperation with the Lawrence Livermore Laboratory Technology Training Program, offers its students training, experience, job access upon graduation, and up-to-date equipment in classrooms. Diablo Valley Enterprises functions as a student club (Diablo Valley College Electronics Club) and is earning enough to purchase nearly $50,000 worth of equipment for the college's electronics department. The students do earn pocket money for their efforts, but their ultimate payoff comes when they are ready for the outside job market.

Another source of valuable education is available through special seminars offered by colleges, universities, and computer businesses. One example is the annual Microcomputers and High Technology in Vocational Education Conference, sponsored by the Vocational Studies Center of the University of Wisconsin–Madison and some twenty-six educational entities. More than two dozen (out of a total of several hundred) industrial and vocational education information sessions are offered in late summer. Classes, displays, and handouts are featured.

Other forms of self-education include reading magazines and books.

High tech is coming of age so fast that it takes a lot of reading to keep up. An early start won't hurt.

Financial Aid

If the education you need cannot be supported entirely by family resources, do not abandon your hopes and plans.

With a little perseverance, financial aid in the form of scholarships, loans, and various combinations of work and study are available to you.

College costs, which include tuition, fees, room, board, books, personal expenses, and travel, may be met by honor awards or needs scholarships and grants.

The first place to inquire is the financial aid office of the school you plan to attend. They will help you file applications for Pell Grant and other federal programs, for state programs, for institutional and private scholarships. Frequently aid is packaged with a combination of grants, low-interest student loans, and work if you qualify for these resources.

If you want a four-year technology education, be sure to consider cooperative programs, which alternate a semester on campus with periods of employment. Many companies also assist with the final two years of education for an employee who holds an associate (two-year) degree. Combining education and experience in this way has proved invaluable for many technology workers.

Chapter VI

What Do You Need to Know?

In a very real way, the knowledge that you need to prepare for a computer technician career must be practical and geared to the real world.

Simply, that means that you must know how to do what needs to be done. You must have specific hands-on skills.

Let's look at some specifics.

At the heart of what you need to know is an understanding of electricity—what it is, how electric current flows in a circuit, what the relationship is between current, voltage, and resistance. You need to know how electricity is produced and to understand alternating current, direct current, generators, and batteries of all types.

You need to learn why Ohm's law is so important to any work with electronics.

Series and parallel circuits must become more than just words to you. Voltage drops, complex circuitry, basic coil action in electronic circuits, types and uses of coils, Lenz's Law and Kirchhoff's Voltage Law must also be added to your list.

The how-to's of capacitors, transistors, and resistors are important parts of your learning. You must know how they are made, how they are used, how they relate to each other, what theories govern their work, how color coding enables you to know their functions, and more.

Integrated circuits and printed-circuit boards will be vital parts of your new knowledge. How these discoveries have launched the high-technology boom and what technicians need to know in repairing and understanding their functions are crucial to computer technician careers.

You will study in depth periodic waveforms, pulses, time constants, and how to observe and measure waveforms in circuitry by using oscilloscopes.

The use of signals in controlling of power, switching operations, relay

COURTESY COMPUTER AND BUSINESS EQUIPMENT MANUFACTURERS ASSOCIATION

Close-up of the integrated monitor portion of a microcomputer, with high-voltage and deflection circuits visible at the top.

circuitry, regulated power supplies, amplifier circuits, and oscillators are all among the basic electronics study that leads you to specific applications and understanding of computer function.

Computer technicians not only need to know how to repair and rework computer elements but also must have a knowledge of computer use and computer programming, because they must be able to test and validate computer functions as they perform their work. They must be able to check them out on their own.

Head knowledge will include basic computer arithmetic including binary numbers, hexadecimal, digital codes, digital logic circuits, boolean alebra, the flow of data through the computer, and types of computer memories.

You will need to know computer input/output information and how it relates to peripheral or accessory equipment. The interactions of computers with display screens, printers, modems, remote terminals, and color equipment are all part of this understanding of peripherals.

Knowing how to convert analog to digital and vice versa will aid in your understanding of data manipulation.

Another key part of your study will deal with the most powerful kind of electronics component—the microprocessor, the tiny chip (usually made of silicon) that is the basis of the microcomputer or personal computer. The applications or uses of microcomputers are growing daily. To keep pace, you will need to study continually.

Every aspect of computers will come alive to you as you pursue the why's and how's of input/output ports, interface circuits, memories and how they are used, and register transfers of software. You will need to know programming languages and how they are used by computing machines. You will need to understand how software is developed. You will need to be familiar with software tools such as assemblers, compilers, editors, interpreters, and operating systems.

How do computers store information? A technician must have a complete understanding of disks including hard, floppy, and mini, as well as tape cartridge systems, disk drives, and transfer of information.

Troubleshooting equipment and how to use it, the importance of "handshaking," logical approaches to computer repair, understanding of the power of computers, programming, computer capabilities, and debugging programs are all part of the knowledge that allows you to move deeper and deeper into the heart of a computer. Needless to say, the only way you can do this is to have your own (preferably build your own) computer or have total access to a computer as you learn. The more time you spend with it, the more you will learn.

Computer power is worthwhile only if you learn to control it. You will learn how to expand its memory capacity by installing chips.

As you set out to prepare yourself for a computer technician career, you need to remember that there are two ways to learn. "You can learn *about* computers. Or you can learn *with* computers," says Quint Morris, Oxnard College instructor and computer entrepreneur. "It is infinitely better to learn *with* computers. For technicians especially, hands-on training is an absolute necessity."

Technical Standards

Specific personal and technological standards must be met by students who wish to pursue service technician careers, according to the Computer and Business Equipment Manufacturers Association.

COURTESY DIGITAL EQUIPMENT CORPORATION

Computer users want the computer up and running as quickly as possible. They watch anxiously as the technician does keyboard repair. Note that the technician traveled through snow to make this repair call.

Those standards cover a broad base of personal skills, interpersonal relations and communications, mathematics, basic mechanics, soldering, mechanical drawing, electronics, electrical symbols and diagrams, tools and test equipment, parts handling, and reporting and record-keeping administration.

Personal Skills

Repair services must be accomplished by a computer service technician in a successful professional manner even when the user (customer) is very angry or when the repair necessitates working in a cramped or awkward position. Further, technicians must show reliability in accurately carrying out complex and specific steps in a long adjustment procedure or working alone for a full eight-hour work day.

Necessary communication skills must include the ability to use clear, concise, and technically accurate language to explain procedures to a co-worker, answer questions, relate to sales people, explain conflicts to a supervisor, or prepare job applications and résumés.

Math and Mechanics

Demonstrable ability in accurate addition, subtraction (including binary, octal, and hexadecimal), multiplication, division, calculating powers of ten, measuring (English or metric), and conversion of numbers from one base to another must also be achieved while in school.

Basic mechanical ability includes such things as adjusting solenoids, micro switches, tensions on belt and chain drives, and parts lubrication. There must be an understanding of levers, gears, chains, sprockets, belts, and pulleys and how they are used for mechanical advantage and speed of motion.

Identification of defective parts means also knowing the cause and result of their condition. That would cover broken or frayed wires, misshapen shafts, relay contacts, motor components, bushings, gears, sprockets, pulleys, or deformed springs.

Training will include familiarity with the use of all types of screws including machine, sheet metal, fine metal, self-tapping, coarse thread, thumbscrews, setscrews, capscrews, and various heads—hex, Allen, flat, fillister, and Phillips.

Pins (spiral, dowel, tapered, roll, cotter), keys (square, woodruff), rings (truarc, E- and G-), and nuts (hex, jam, castellated, wing, cap, thumb, stop, tinnerman) are all part of the technician's knowledge. He or she must understand the problems that result from stripped or cross-threaded screws and nuts.

There's more to soldering than first meets the eye. Using an isolated soldering iron, vacuum and desoldering tool, solder braid, heat sinks, flux cleaner, different wattages of soldering irons, different fluxes and solders, and tip cleaning equipment are all necessary. Removing and replacing an integrated circuit on a printed-circuit board, keeping the foil intact, preventing burn spots or cold solder joints, and insuring that the IC tests properly as well as using all tools safely and effectively are part and parcel of the technician's skills.

Understanding and using mechanical drawings, electrical symbols, block and timing diagrams, and schematics are essential.

A computer technician must be well versed in basic electronics and be able to solve multiple electrical circuit functions using Ohm's Law, measure currents and voltages in AC circuits in a variety of circumstances, and define common base, common emitter, and common collector transistor circuit characteristics. He/she must also be able to wire and verify the input and output circuitry of logic gates, using truth tables.

Hand tools, power tools, and electronic test equipment are the tools with which the computer technician works.

Among the hand tool uses are tightening (box and open-end wrenches, hex wrenches, ratchet-drive socket wrenches, slip-joint pliers, needle-nose pliers, screwdrivers); cutting (hacksaws, files and file card, wire cutters, wire strippers, abrasive cloths), drilling (drills), measuring (dial indicators, thermometers, temperature gauges, feeler gauges), soldering (differing wattages of soldering irons, heat sinks, solder braid, desoldering tools, tip cleaning equipment), and other specialized functions (center punches, O-ring removal tool, hammers, mirrors, spring hooking tools, pin extractors for electrical plugs and sockets).

Power tools include electric drills and electric grinders. Integral to the work are electronic test instruments including oscilloscopes, volt-ohmmeters, digital voltmeters, and ammeters.

PHOTO BY JEAN SPENCER

An IC remover is used to remove an integrated circuit from a computer.

Parts handling is another key function performed by computer technicians. Varied items such as shafts, bearings, circuit boards, glass items, lubricants, small electronic parts, screws, bolts, pins, keys, rings, rollers, seals, gaskets, and plastic parts must all be stored and located easily when needed.

Alphabetic and numeric filing, adding or purging data, completing time and activity reports, ordering parts, and keeping machine service history logs with correct technical terms are important elements in the reports and record-keeping that are part of the technician's job. Map reading, too, is important for locating a customer's business and pinpointing the best route to a given address.

Chapter VII

Other Pathways to Your Goal

Military Training

An education resource that many young people overlook is military service.

Consider for a moment what the Air Force offers in the way of technical training. The Air Force operates one of the largest first-rate technical training programs in the world. It ranges all the way from free, no-obligation aptitude testing at the high school level to associate in applied science, bachelor's, and doctoral degree programs.

Gone are the days when enlisting was easy, at least as far as the Air Force is concerned. Qualification standards have been increased by 40 percent, and applicants are still up by 150 percent during the past two years. The training and education the Air Force offers is first-rate, and the people they are seeking must be first-rate, too.

If you qualify, you can be sure of computer technology training that will be respected and in demand. It will not cost you dollars as other schooling does, but it will cost you at least a four-year commitment.

What does it take to qualify for the Air Force these days?

A strong basic education is the key. Mathematics is the first requirement, with sciences a close second. English and literature are stressed, and a GPA (grade point average) of 3.75 or 4.0 is really what they want.

"Everybody wants to get into computers these days," one recruiting officer said. "But they don't want to study math, and that is absolutely necessary. They must have a good understanding of math."

Math includes algebra, trigonometry, geometry, calculus. Solid subjects may not be easy. Mastering them requires ambition, discipline, and determination, but the rewards that come with that kind of mastery pay off over many years to come.

Knowing the requirements early in your education years allows you to prepare adequately and to set yearly goals for yourself. That is important.

Another important thing to know is that acceptance for Air Force training includes waiting for a year or more once you have a job reservation for the training field that you want to pursue. You have a choice—but you also must meet high standards and plan ahead.

The first step toward Air Force enlistment is taking the Armed Services Vocational Aptitude Battery (ASVAB). This aptitude testing is designed to determine your special capabilities. It is offered free of charge and with no obligation, and you may use the results in any way you like.

If you qualify, and discussions with recruiters have given you specific information about programs that will meet their needs and your expectations, you will then explore the Guaranteed Training Enlistment Program. Or, if specific openings are not available, the Delayed Enlistment Program should be considered. Another, more generalized option entails enlisting in a specific Aptitude Index such as Electronics or Mechanical. You must also be aware that passing a physical examination is necessary. Be cautious in signing your enlistment agreement, and read it carefully. Because so many enlistees want to get into computer training, some effort may be made to switch you into another field.

Six weeks of basic training is the first step. It's tough, but good experience. Learning *why* to do things is an important part of that training. Learning to follow instructions, help others, and work in a group is the kind of discipline that will work for you. After that, your schooling will begin.

Computer Technology is taught at the USAF Technical Training School at Sheppard Air Force Base in Texas. Computer Systems is taught at Keesler AFB in Mississippi.

All airmen and airwomen are encouraged to enroll in the Community College of the Air Force. The CCAF program encourages enlisted people to combine accredited Air Force technical instruction with voluntary off-duty education for a complete and balanced study program. This is viewed as preparation for leadership. All major Air Force Technical Schools are accredited schools, and the CCAF has the authority to grant the associate in applied science degree. Even if you do not complete the degree program during your tour of duty, the transcript record of your completed classes is valuable because accredited, transferable academic achievement will count in the civilian world as well.

Electronic Computer Technology is but one of many electronics and telecommunications computer-related specialized training fields. Finding your place is as important to the Air Force as it is to you—perhaps more so.

The entire Space Shuttle program is requiring thousands of trained and skilled people. The opportunity for learning and participating is there for the individual; the necessity for discipline, dependability, and reliability in its vast assemblage of people power is a national requirement. Vandenberg Air Force Base in California is the location and focus of important energy. With the Air Force as the nation's first line of defense, the necessity for first-rate people becomes clear.

You learn by doing in the Air Force. The instruction is not just theory. The opportunity to apply the principles learned in class is an integral part of the training. The "why" and "how" are reinforced. That meets Air Force needs; it not only makes you valuable during your military career, but it returns you to the civilian job market with a usable skill. Other thousands find the training, work, and opportunity so rewarding that they make the Air Force their long-term career.

Computer technicians who have been trained in the military possess the experience that many employers want. Experience reflects know-

COURTESY VENTURA COUNTY *STAR FREE PRESS*

An assembler inserts a board edge connector.

how and follow-through. It is in demand. Conversely, washing out of the military carries a negative implication. Most private and public employers are looking for indications that you will do a good job for them.

Apprenticeship

Although apprenticeship is a training method prevalent in some other skilled career fields, it is rarely found in computer technology.

Working Up the Company Ladder

The computer industry does start entry-level workers as assemblers. This work generally requires a hands-on worker to be familiar with only a specific part assembly function. Assembling is repetitive work and can be boring. Pay can range from the minimum wage to several dollars an hour higher depending on the complexity of the task and length of employment.

Some assembly workers, especially if they combine after-hours schooling with their job, can work up to testing, inspection, or quality assurance. Knowledge is the key to upward mobility. There is less and less job opportunity for unskilled or semiskilled workers, and education becomes a must, especially in technology careers.

Many companies like to promote from within. Some computer-trained personnel have chosen to enter employment with a particular company as a receptionist, for instance, to be on the inside and ready to move up at the first opportunity. Generally, that is a possibility that you should discuss with the personnel office at the beginning.

There are big advantages if you can start with an employer who offers company training. Not only are you receiving your education at no cost and earning while you learn, but you are also certain of your future employment once you are trained successfully.

Radio, TV, and Electronic Technicians

A significant number of today's computer technicians, particularly in industry, started as radio, television, or electronic technicians.

As this booming new industry began coming of age, they were on the scene and were often either required to learn the new technology or in a position to try working with it on an experimental basis.

Computer technology is a natural progression as new areas open up for electronic technicians who may have reached a dead end in previous work. Their electronic orientation allows them to jump into computer technology and grow with current breakthroughs.

Electronics background is the only way to get into the computer field. Electronic technicians and computer technicians are closely related by virtue of the skills they must possess. In some areas, electronic technician training is the only available or most available educational choice. Some electronic technician programs of instruction include computer technology as one of the specialized focuses. As education continues to grow with the high-technology field, more and more specialized computer technology programs will emerge.

Chapter VIII

How to Test Yourself

Is the world of computers so exciting to you that you involve yourself with them at every opportunity?

Are you reading every book, magazine, and news article that you can get hold of, comparing and analyzing information?

Do you have access to a personal computer, either at home or at school, and take every opportunity to use it?

As a hobby, have you been building small electronic projects, learning to solder, fixing things that require fixing?

Do you think math and science are fun?

Do you like to know WHY things work or don't work? Why things are alike or different? Why some solutions to problems are better than others?

Are you interested in improving things, in making them work better?

Do you have curiosity and imagination?

Do you have the ability to break down a complicated problem into several simple ones in order to find a solution? Can you analyze?

Are you resourceful? Determined? Patient? Persistent?

Do you have drive and stick-to-it-iveness? Do you dislike monotony?

What are your values? Is working within a team of high-tech professionals in order to help shape tomorrow of high interest to you?

Do you like the challenge of work that demands your best efforts? Are you motivated? Goal-directed?

Do you want to continue to learn throughout your adult life? Are your study habits good?

If you answer yes to those questions, you already have part of the answer as to whether being a computer technician might be the career for you.

But only part.

Are you building a solid foundation in math? Do you have an A or B average in algebra, trigonometry, calculus, geometry? In the sciences? In literature?

Yes answers to these tell you that you are getting the grounding, the foundation that you need to keep up with the rapidly growing high-technology world.

Aptitude Testing

Counselors at your high school, at community colleges, and at four-year colleges may give you aptitude tests designed to help you discover your fields of interest.

One such test is the COPSystem Interest Inventory. If you take this interest inventory, you indicate your likes and dislikes as they relate to 168 different career situations.

After the results are tabulated, you can see your strengths and weaknesses in fourteen major occupational groupings, including professional technology and skilled technology. Your interest profile is then compared with those of others at your educational level to give you an idea of how your responses may be interpreted and which areas you might do well to explore.

ASVAB Testing

Another testing avenue is the ASVAB or Armed Services Vocational Aptitude Battery. This written test may be scheduled through your local Air Force recruiter. There is no charge or obligation, although it often is taken as the first step toward enlistment. You may use the results in any way that is helpful to you.

The ASVAB will give you results in the areas of mechanics, administrative fields, general occupational fields, and electronics.

Testing Not Always Needed

Many counselors do not recommend aptitude testing. You may agree with them.

Large group aptitude tests have questionable validity, according to Dale Ackerman, head counselor at Westlake High School. If students do not take it seriously, the results are not valid, he feels. The tests are very broad in nature, and the results are fairly predictable. They also are more likely to reflect a given moment rather than provide a basis for long-range planning.

One-to-one talks are much more indicative, Ackerman feels, because the level of commitment is more apt to surface. A good career goal, he points out, has to fit the rest of a student's personality. For instance, a desire to be a pilot or a computer programmer without a strong interest in math is not realistic. Liking to do numbers "by myself" gives a much better indication.

Ackerman has two questions that he considers the best barometers: What do you like to do? and What do you do best? "If you answer those two questions honestly and find that the answers are in sync with each other, that gives a pretty good indication," he believes.

Knowing Yourself

Knowing yourself is an important part of preparing yourself for a career. That includes your abilities and your weaknesses as well as your strengths.

Assessing your personal work habits will be important to your employer and will play a large role in your career success or failure.

Among the important things to consider are your dependability, health, honesty, perseverance, and personal appearance.

Knowing what is expected of you, having the ability to manage time and materials efficiently, and being able to adjust to various work situations are qualities that will play an important role.

Can you get along with people of varying personalities? Can you work both independently and as a team member, with some understanding of when each is appropriate? Will you be loyal to the organization you work for? How are you at working under pressure? Can you adjust to varying work situations?

Are you capable of making decisions? Are initiative and imagination among your talents?

Considering those qualities and questions will give you some insight into what an employer will expect of you and what you can bring to the job in addition to technical skills.

Work habits play an important role in job success. The better you know yourself and build in your own success potential, the better. When your employer rates you on these qualities, you will be a step ahead.

Your school years are not only the years of learning subject material but also the years of developing good work habits, outlook on life, and interpersonal skills. Those attributes should develop as you mature, enabling you to bring your best habits to your career along with your academic and technical skills.

Part of knowing yourself includes the ability to listen to parents and friends. They can be helpful in giving you additional understanding of yourself from their perspective. Parents, older friends, and currently employed technicians often have a view of the work world that can prove highly profitable to you. Listen to them, and listen to your own feelings and attitudes as well. You must make the decision on your life's work.

Knowing the demands of your career goal and knowing your ability to meet them will give you self-confidence. For instance, requirements for this field include a strong technical knowledge and skills in electro-mechanics, electronics, diagnostics, logic, and troubleshooting. Are you interested and on your way to mastering them?

Technicians must also be expert in the use of required tools, meters, and electronic test equipment. How do you measure up?

Applicants for entry-level jobs may have to pass tests measuring mechanical aptitude, knowledge of electricity and electronics, manual dexterity, and general intelligence. They may also have to pass a physical examination. Cultivating the ability to know yourself and to know how you are likely to perform on any of those tests will give you confidence, even if tests make you nervous.

Counseling

Chances are that you will make your own career choice. The days seem to be gone when someone else did it for you, although staying in tune with the job *needs* of employers and the educational requirements of schools and colleges is a good idea.

It is important for you to know your own mind, but even knowing yourself is not easy. It does not come without some direction, some influence from others.

Industry leaders see five possible areas of influence that may help you to chart your future, to understand yourself and your career interests.

Those areas of influence include career counseling, family friends and neighbors, teaching advice, self-analysis, and general sources of information.

If you are being turned on to career choice possibilities by your school counselor, you are fortunate. A good career counselor can give you practical insights, help you to see your future, and provide some solid feet-on-the-ground skills such as job interview techniques and résumé writing.

They can, through such aids as the Gould Career Center informational film strips, give you introductory looks at the occupations you are considering and give you a clearer view of the realities of the world of work.

With industry now recognizing the necessity of working more closely with schools and colleges to provide the kind of trained labor pool they will need in the years to come, more helps are on the horizon for you, the worker of the future.

For instance, the Job Shadowing program instituted in the three colleges of the Ventura County Community College District in California is bringing together college counselors and leaders in Ventura County industry. With industry leaders telling counselors in round-table discussions exactly what they will need in the way of trained workers, and with the counselors following up with on-site industry visits and tours, the counselors are being equipped to provide more accurate information and understanding to their students.

Even the knowledge and information available from a skilled counselor, however, will not help if you do not take the initiative to seek it out. Asking questions is the best way to locate the counselor who can prove most helpful. Asking questions is also the best way to ferret out the information you want.

Even the most valuable counselor rarely has time to chase after students. Perhaps that is why a recent survey shows that students in technical fields rarely remembered any significant career counseling at the junior high level, only 30 percent recalled any in high school, and only 19 percent felt that career counseling had influenced their actual career. The bleak funding situation in education does curtail the number of counselors and, therefore, the amount of counseling time offered. Asking questions is the best way to get what you need and the counseling you need. Even an extremely busy counselor is more likely to be helpful if you show initiative and ask for specific information.

Reforms in education and closer alliances between business and industry such as the Job Shadowing programs should enable you to get more up-to-date information, and the trend should increase.

In the same survey, the influence of family, friends, and neighbors proved to be the outstanding influence, affecting 96 percent of the undergraduate technical and engineering students polled. More than half—53 percent—credited the family as the major influence. Fathers were specified by far as the family member having the most influence— 53 percent—and the combined guidance of both parents showed a significant percentage. Major types of advice included interest, ability, security, and money.

High school and university teachers seemed to have significant influence during students' education years, although only 28 percent of students said they took advantage of, and used, that advice. The academic subjects themselves appeared to have the most influence, with math, physics, and drafting leading for technical-minded students.

The survey's strongest indication was that the student's self-analysis (including self-comparisons of ability and interest in the subject matter) greatly determined their future. In other words, they thought about what they wanted to do. They assessed their strengths and weaknesses, their interests and their performance. Originators of the survey believe that that indicates a mature seriousness of purpose. Eighty-five percent of the students were interested in problem-solving that produced visible results; 89 percent enjoyed problem-solving that utilized mental and handwork together. Note that work can be, and is, enjoyable. Analyzing yourself to discover the type of work that is most enjoyable to you will set you on a course that is infinitely more satisfying than merely drifting into a career.

Several other sources were designated as helpful in the survey. Among them were job forecast information and career guidance literature (such as you are now reading), college catalogs, magazines, Museum of Science and Industry, university or college visits, and newspaper want ads.

Chapter IX

Opportunities for Women

Technician jobs are often seen as masculine or men's work simply because men have been doing them longer or because they are machine-related and may require dirty hands.

Technical requirements, however, are not related to sex. Many women are proving that technician's work is anybody's work.

One thing women need to remember is that technology or technician education provides them with salable skills. Those skills provide economic mobility, and, an important point, they are portable. If a woman needs to relocate because of a personal or family situation, she will be able to do so with relative ease. She can expect to find her skills in demand in a new location or, equally important, after an absence of a few years if she elects to take time out to concentrate on children.

As the demand for high-tech employees continues to rise, transforming society, the demand for computer technicians will grow. Current demographic trends show a smaller pool of skilled male applicants. As in other historical times, women will step in to provide the additional source of labor. Furthermore, women are more likely to have developed good study habits and to have achieved superior high school records. Building on those will enable women to become highly qualified technicians and technologists. National test scores show that men and women can be equally competent or incompetent. Analysis at some engineering schools shows women getting the best marks in their classes.

If there is a problem with a too-small number of women in technician and technology positions, it is no longer that they are not wanted. Despite efforts to do so, industry has not yet been able to attract as many women as it needs. As young women begin to realize that they will spend most of their adult lives in the work force, preparing themselves for work that is interesting and satisfying will be beneficial for both themselves and industry. It pays women both in dollars and in job

COURTESY MOUNT SAN ANTONIO COLLEGE

Students run a diagnostic test to evaluate a problem.

satisfaction to train for a career in a field that is interesting, important to society, and well compensated.

Technician training may also be available through night classes at a local community college or technical school, thus proving helpful to a woman who is seeking upward mobility or entrance into a new technical career while still meeting current daytime responsibilities.

Many women will continue to give priority to their personal lives, and a well-chosen career will help toward that goal. During both the study-preparation years and the working years in the field of computer technology, a satisfactory balance of work and personal goals should be possible.

Opportunities

"We hire talent."

Those are the words of Rod Franz, a civil service computer technology supervisor, responding to the question of opportunities for women who are interested in pursuing careers as computer technicians.

On at least one of three shifts in his operation, the male-female ratio is 50-50. That is not surprising because federal law requires equal opportunity on the basis of sex as well as for minorities. Government and educational entities are required by that law to make every effort to open hiring opportunities to women and minority workers.

What may be even more interesting to young women is that, accord-

A computer technician solves a mechanical problem.

ing to Franz, "Private industry is hiring women and minorities away from us. And, since private industry pays more, it succeeds."

Managers in the rapidly growing third-party computer service field are quick to agree. They strongly encourage women to train for technician jobs, and they actively recruit female technicians across the country. They believe that this career field offers a wealth of potential for women.

A recent study by the DeVry Institute of Technology that involved 100 employment managers in the Chicago area showed, too, that the number of women entering the field of computer science is on the rise, and that those already in the field are moving up. A significant increase in the number of women in technical positions over the past five years was reported by 68 percent of the managers. Overall, companies reported a 20 percent increase in the number of women hired.

The DeVry study showed a strong willingness on the part of employment managers to hire qualified women. In jobs traditionally considered male positions, the stereotype is quickly being eroded. Companies want to hire well-qualified people, people who know what they are doing, according to the study. Personnel managers interviewed ranked specific skills and education as the primary qualifications for employment; and, of the two, skills were clearly preferred.

"We hire talent" are three key words. Employers want workers who are skilled and experienced on the particular equipment or in the specific area of work where their need is.

A real key to becoming "talent" in this field often depends on choices made by young women in their junior high, high school, and college years.

Those are the years of schooling when choice becomes possible. That choice may be as broad as the number and degree of difficulty of math classes scheduled versus classes in other solid and/or elective subjects. Or it might be more subtle and relate to decisions to put more or less effort into learning the subject material in one class or another.

The truth is that when it comes to careers in computer technology at the technician level, a demonstrated competence in mathematics is the base on which much rests. That is even more true at the advanced levels that technology-minded women may want to achieve.

The accomplishments of girls in the early years of schooling are very impressive. This early competence would seem to indicate that they would also do well in algebra, geometry, and higher forms of mathematics when they reach junior high and high school age. The fact is that many young women do exactly that: They choose to study math and do very well with it both in the classroom and in their later lives.

Yet many others do not try to master the more abstract concepts of mathematics, and their talent is left lying dormant.

This is a crucial point.

With high technology careers open to talented women, there must be *prepared* talented women to apply and to get them. The study of mathematics is integral to the preparation demanded.

Earl Estes, math instructor at Oxnard College, frequently works with women students who want to overcome an earlier aversion to math. He feels that their anxiety often rests on misconceptions. "Nobody keeps all those numbers in their head," he points out. "Math is primarily based on understanding the concepts. Learning *how* to move the numbers around and learning what the numbers represent are two important breakthroughs in conquering math. Women can do it as well as men."

Although engineering and technical fields have been dominated by men for many years, the high-technology boom offers special opportunities for women in a number of ways.

As is the case with pioneering situations, there are fewer stereotypes from the past to hold you back. Many of the jobs opening up in the field of computer technology have never existed before. The person with the talent is going to have the best opportunity to use it.

For some women, learning word processing and other new office technology has been a natural progression in upward mobility from the traditional office jobs of the past. Mastering word processing, data processing, or information systems may launch capable women into other (and more financially rewarding) technology. Women are discovering that continuing their education to keep pace with the times brings mental stimulation as well as greater pay benefits.

Role Models and Mentors

Seeking out role models to learn from is a good way to improve your chances.

A role model is someone you admire, someone you can learn from, someone who has already done what you would like to do. You may watch her, talk with her, perhaps even visit her at work to get an idea of what she does and why she does it. Her inspiration, in various ways, will give you the ideas and the assurance that you need to get started. "If she can do it, I can too," is a good motto for you.

When looking for a role model, keep in mind that, while it is good to have a woman, you may want to use a man for your role model. That may especially be true if you want to break into a technical field that would be a "first" for women employees. Or in a very new aspect of high technology where everyone is pioneering, you will certainly want to learn from whoever you can.

Keep in mind, too, that you should have several role models. They may be of both sexes, of varying approaches and capabilities. If you continue to ask yourself the question, "What can I learn from them?" you will begin to build your own expertise. You may learn a hands-on skill from one, a personal relations approach from another, a method of study from another, and so on. You will be preparing yourself with a unique collection of skills.

At some point in time, you may be fortunate enough to have a mentor. Mentoring as a career development strategy, according to consultant Diane Moore, is a way to get ahead. It involves a working relationship with someone several rungs up who reaches down and gives you a hand. It is especially effective for women who fear success or who are hesitatnt to use their intelligence for fear of appearing masculine.

Mentoring is a positive way to increase your determination, your confidence, your energy, your skills, and your support. Some companies have formal mentoring systems. Other arrangements are more individual.

It takes some initiative to form a mentor-protégée relationship. This relationship is closer than a teacher-trainee relationship. Mentoring involves feedback, encouragement, understanding.

It is important to agree up front what the clear expectations are, what the roles are, and what the duration should be (six months is often about right).

Support Systems

Many women are finding that other business contacts, professional women's groups, conferences, seminars, family, and friends can offer various helpful support systems. Community colleges such as Oxnard College and California Lutheran College have yearly Women's Day events featuring as many as fifty-six separate skill and personal-growth workshops. Those events also attract other women who may be helpful and encouraging to you as you plan your career.

Chapter **X**

Equipment, Tools, and Computer Environments

Working with computers sounds glamorous. It has an exciting, high-tech ring to it.

Men and women preparing for computer technician careers with sound vocational training background and the required aptitudes of accuracy, detail orientation, and ability to think in the same logical steps as the computer will find challenge and career growth potential in the field. Their friends and relatives may admire, respect, or envy them.

Yet, computer industry work is not for everyone.

Stress

Computer work environments are stressful. The primary reason relates to the computer itself. "Downtime"—when there is a malfunction and everything comes to a halt—is very expensive. Estimated costs run from $200 to $400 a minute. All workers on the scene feel a sense of frustration and urgency until the computer is operational again and work can proceed on schedule.

Computer service technicians are the ones looked to in those exasperating situations to make everything right again and to do it as fast as possible. If you can bring calm as well as expertise to the situation, you will be rewarded, but if an uptight situation sets your nerves on edge, you may want to think twice about planning to spend your working hours in a stressful environment.

Because computer response times are very fast—and getting faster all the time—that speed is another cause of stress that affects those who work with them. Computer speeds are far faster than those of humans, and yet human beings attempt to keep pace.

Computers and related equipment require a relatively dust-free environment. For that reason, computer centers have no windows. The closed environment, with artificial lighting, may have difficult and subtle side effects on workers who spend eight-hour shifts in one place. It is more likely to affect computer operators than technicians, who will probably be moving from place to place. Temperature controls are important to the operation of computers, and workers must adjust to the cooler temperature needed for the computer to function properly.

The constant need for problem-solving is a final stress point to consider. Questions such as "Why is the computer down?," "Why is this program not working?," "Why are output data not correct?," "Why have we lost the data?," or "Does that mean we have to reenter the entire day's work?" are only a few of the upsetting problems that confront computer operators and computer technicians frequently. They require immediate analysis and corrective measures. The pressure to find the problem and solve it efficiently does cause a stressful and anxious atmosphere.

Personal aptitudes become important. Whereas anxiety and pressure cause some people discomfort, other people thrive in such situations. Challenges cause them to rise to the occasion. Their adrenalin flows. Nothing is more interesting to them than making things right again. Is that your attitude?

The word "computer" may sound like an all-encompassing term.

Within the industry, however, you must learn quickly that there are many kinds of computers, many specialized functions, and a vocabulary that must be learned.

Hardware is the term used to describe computers and computer equipment.

Among the types of hardware that technicians must be familiar with are mainframes (large installations tailored to particular industry needs), minicomputers (mid-size installations), and micro systems. Microcomputers are often called personal or home computers. Even though they look small and compact, usually fitting on a desk or table top in about the same space as a typewriter, they are quite powerful and can accomplish complex functions that a few years ago required a large room full of equipment.

Computers, or CPU's (central processing unit), process or perform all of the calculations, filing, word processing, organizing, analyzing, and other functions that any given user or employer needs to accomplish.

Hardware also refers to special-purpose systems and input-output equipment, usually called peripherals. Peripherals may include disk drives, printers, and monitors. Communications interface equipment such as modems (telephone connections) are becoming increasingly important.

Disk drives accept the program or information disks that tell the computer what to do and/or what to save.

Printers, on command, print out on paper the information that has been processed in the computer.

Monitors, or CRT's (cathode ray tubes), look very much like a television screen and give the user a convenient place to view whatever information is being used.

Modems allow the computer on site to be connected by telephone lines to other computers in distant locations. Network is a term that describes the use of modems and other long-distance interconnecting equipment. Establishing and working with the networks is a fast-growing and important facet of work for some computer technicians.

Basically, then, hardware refers to all the pieces of equipment that you can see and touch.

Software, on the other hand, is the term used to describe packages of programmed instructions. Disks are the most frequently used type of software. They may be hard disks or floppy disks. They may be of different sizes. Yet each has inscribed in its memory a complete set of instructions for carrying out one or more particular functions.

Some computers may be programmed by using tape cassettes. Still others have been designed to be used with cartridges. However, the common element is that each of these types of software carries the instructions that the computer needs to function.

Those who know how to use software programs are considered computer-literate. Computer-literate does not mean knowing how to program; it does mean being able to use programs and operate the equipment.

Software is also used for storing data and new programs. Blanks are used to "save" new information that is entered into the computer. A great deal of information can be saved on one blank disk.

The best way to describe a disk is that it is like a phonograph record. However, the actual surface is very fragile. Floppy disks are made of mylar and are encased in a square, almost paper-thin cover. Only a tiny section of the disk is visible through a small opening. It is very important never to touch the actual disk, allow dirt to contaminate it, or damage it in any way. That is a small price to pay compared to the problems that ensue when the computer "crashes" or fails to operate because of damage or malfunction.

Although computer technicians must be familiar with all phases of the computer and be able to use it, they rarely are much concerned with the output of work or the functions of specific programs.

Technicians are involved with computer services. There are hundreds, perhaps thousands, of jobs that technicians may perform. Some are involved with the design and installation of computer systems and communications interface networks. Some do computer system troubleshooting when there is a problem. Some do preventive maintenance. Some use computers in the pursuit of other technician tasks. Some are involved with building various types of computerized equipment. The variety of work gives you an idea how may specialties are emerging and how important it is to decide which kind of technician you would like to be. Over your lifetime, however, you will probably have several different technician jobs.

All computer technicians must be familiar with tools. They must know how to use them, when to use them, and why they are used. They must know which tool is needed for a particular function.

Computer technician tool kits, reflecting the greater sophistication of the computer world in general, often are housed in injection molded attaché cases. It is possible to purchase a kit that is designed to cover all the basics, but technicians usually add new tools to meet their particular needs.

Among the versatile and functional tools you will encounter are the following:

    logic monitor and probe
    circuit board puller
    DIP insertion tool
    extractor pliers
    wire strippers
    soldering iron, low leakage, 3 tips
    soldering aid, fork and reamer
    soldering aid, brush and knife
    solder remover braid, 2 each
    solder, pocket pack
    solder sucker
    screwdrivers
    nut drivers
    hemostat
    pushbutton knife
    pocket magnifier
    lead forming tool
    inspection mirror
    disposable penlight
    thin needlenose pliers
    short-nose tipcutter pliers

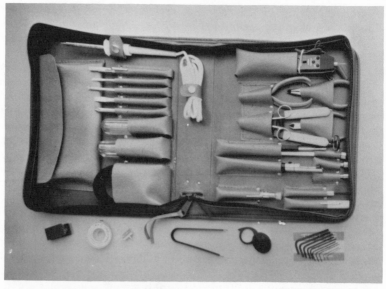

COURTESY JENSEN TOOLS

Computer technician kits are light and easy to carry.

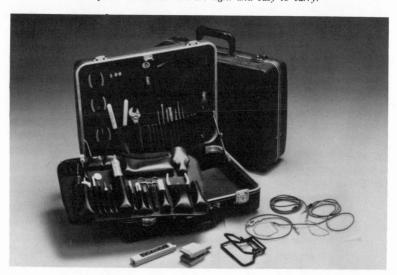

COURTESY JENSEN TOOLS

Jensen's de luxe computer technician tool kit is carried in an attaché case.

semiflush cutter pliers
slotted blade screwdrivers, 1/8", 3/16", 1/4"
Phillips screwdriver blades, #0, #1, #2
screwdriver handle for blades
screwdriver extension blade, 4"
wire wrap/unwrap tool
adjustable wrench, 6"
antistatic work station

Printed-circuit board kits may also include:

reverse action tweezers
digital probe
drill, cordless mini
X-acto knife with blade
diagonal cutter pliers, 4 1/4"
wire stripper/cutter
wire wrap/unwrap tool
multiposition work holder
quick-adjust vise for holding circuit boards
miniature chain-nose pliers

Familiarity with tools can begin as early as you have an interest in them. Discovering the right tool and the appropriate uses of each can be fun as well as practical. Impossible tasks become possible with the right tool and the knowledge that enables you to use it.

Still, familiarity with the tools is only part of your task. You will also need to get acquainted with:

resistors
transistors
EPROMS
IC's or integrated circuits
printed-circuit boards
motherboards
RAMS
capacitors
power supplies
modules, sub-assembly, self-contained
buffers
spoolers
circuits

bus
controller
encoder
field
first generation
flowchart
master control program
matrix (dot matrix)
optical scanner
read
relationship symbols
subroutine
enter
control
escape
error

COURTESY MOUNT SAN ANTONIO COLLEGE

Computer installations are reasonably sterile environments in order to keep dust and contaminants at a minimum.

Environment

Computer environments often require specific measures such as filtered air, positive force ventilation, white lab coats for workers, and sticky mats at the door to pull dust off of workers' shoes.

Cleaning of relays, vacuuming, and dusting are tasks of the technician. Because it is so crucial to the efficient operation of computer systems, technicians must be especially alert to the danger of smoke, fumes, temperature, fan breakdown, humidity, dust, and dirt. Computer environments are set up to alleviate those problems, and the technician is frequently called upon to explain why the controls are so important as well as to repair damage caused when the controls fail.

Computers, especially large computers, do develop heat. In the event of fire, it is highly important to know the right kind of fire extinguisher that may be used and to have it on hand. Halon, with its relatively low toxicity, is the preferred one. It can smother fire without damaging the delicate components of the computer. The lack of residue in the computer is vital. Use of water, carbon dioxide, or powder extinguishers would certainly damage, destroy, or upset delicate electronic equipment.

Special equipment is also needed to monitor power lines and prevent power surges that can cause "glitches," brownouts, or power shutdowns. Backup generators are commonly installed to give workers five or ten extra minutes in the event of a power failure to save current processes. These noninterruptible power supply measures prevent loss of data and costly time.

Chapter XI

Job-finding Techniques

Finding employment as a technician in the computer industry can be a creative challenge.

The industry is "open" in employment opportunities, and there are few fixed patterns so far in career advancement. Even obtaining entry-level positions often is the result of the same kind of creative exploration that excites and attracts people to computers in the first place. It bears repeating that the Information Age is a new frontier, and in that sense many aspects of computer employment are open to enthusiasts, pioneers, and unusual career path approaches.

Absolutely vital to your finding the right first job is your ability to demonstrate to a prospective employer that you really are interested in serving the industry as a computer technician, that you can do the job, and that you can get along with other people on the job.

Success in landing your first job as a computer technician really isn't any different from getting a job in any other field.

Remember that training and promotion opportunities depend on each person's skills, abilities, and aptitudes. Managers and those doing the hiring or promoting look for persons who are at ease with the machine. They look for workers who follow steps of logic just as the computer does. Right from the start, right from your résumé and your interview, you should convince them that you have those qualities. You want them to know that when they choose you for a position and when they invest in you, they will be getting their money's worth.

It may give you an edge if you remember that employers invest more in each employee than the salary they pay. Employers are investing time, training, future planning, and expectations. They have a right to expect a return on their investment. When you have a mind set that realizes this, when you give them evidence that you expect to give them their money's worth, when you give them reason to believe that you really want them to achieve their goals, and when you illustrate those points with an approach that combines personal energy and skill, you will have an advantage in seeking that first job.

Employers are also looking for training that is pertinent to their needs. A good working knowledge of particular equipment will gain you access to one company and not help at another, depending on their specific needs.

High school, community college, or technical school graduates must realize that entry-level jobs in the computer industry can and do open many doors of opportunity for career growth. That first job is only a beginning.

Obstacles are challenges. The first hurdle—and the most difficult one—is getting your foot in the door with the first job. After that, your interest and your skills will have a good chance of taking you where you want to go.

Experience is the single most important quality that you can bring to a prospective employer. If you have put the information in Chapter V to good use, you have experience to offer your first employer. Anything pertaining to computers counts. You are prepared, and now is the time to showcase that experience and let your prospective employer know that you are more than just a warm body. You should also realize that many employers who require "experience" accept formal education as part of that experience. Volunteer work also is of interest.

Because so much of a computer technician's job today depends on problem-solving and specific procedures directly related to an individual firm's computer installation, a new worker must realize that unique skills learned on the job are required. Experience, and learning to make the most of that experience, shows your awareness of this important business principle.

As you begin the process of connecting with your first full-time job, try a systematic approach.

Identify the companies that provide entry-level training, those that hire beginners, those that are currently hiring in your interest area. This research includes checking the help-wanted ads, but it goes far beyond that. Check the phone book yellow pages (start with "Data Processing Equipment"), read the business section of the newspaper to learn of companies relocating or expanding in your area. Be aware of significant businesses through their display advertising in magazines or newspapers. That may lead you to consider another geographic location: more about that later.

As you consider your options, recognize that many large establishments with growing demand for computer personnel may be the ones with opportunities for entry-level training and also career ladders available to beginners. These establishments may include utility companies, defense contractors, manufacturers, and major corporations.

If you are now working part time or in an intern position, find out if your employer has any transfer openings or other suggestions. You may also be able to connect with other business colleagues; contacts do open doors.

Expand your contacts by using networking techniques. Let family, friends, and instructors know that you are interested in a computer technician career. Ask them for a referral to anyone they may know in the field. Attend computer shows and computer-user groups. All of those contacts should be part of a carefully constructed plan to transform yourself from an outsider to a well-informed and well-connected insider.

Persistence pays. You must take the initiative and make your job happen. Even in this field where job opportunities are expected to double, the best jobs will always go to the gogetter.

You may be in the enviable position of having several first jobs to choose from. Or you may, after doing your homework and considering all the factors, turn down your first job offer in favor of waiting for what you consider to be the right job for you.

There is risk in turning down a job offer; there may not be another right away. But there is also risk in accepting a job that may not start you on a good career path. There is no easy way to tell you when to say "yes" and when to say "no." The soundest advice is that you almost always have to compromise because no job is perfect. There are always risks—in life as well as in career choices. But you must be sure that you have given your best thought to the matter and that you have considered all the angles and possibilities.

Early on in your job search, you must decide what you believe would be the ideal job for you. Where do you want to be in five or ten years? That will give you a base against which to weigh the advice and input of others. If you know something would be wrong for you, don't let others sway or manipulate you or make your choices for you. Listen to their advice, accept what seems reasonable, and discard what doesn't fit. Process their input along with your own. Be open to new and profitable ideas, but let decisions be your own. Your interest in computers shows that you have a logical mind. Let that logic work for you as well when it comes to making career decisions.

Later on, choices may revolve around whether to move on to management or remain technical. Fortunately, many companies now realize that technical people should be compensated according to their real worth, and moving into management is no longer necessary for pulling in greater income.

In deciding to seek employment, it is good to realize that the smaller the company, the more hats each employee wears. In a small or medium-size operation, you may have less chance for advancement but more opportunity to manage. On the other hand, if you prefer long-time technical work, you would probably do well to choose a large company.

Being realistic is key to your choice of a career goal. Backing up your goal with the correct foundation classes and personal skills is fundamental. Choosing a goal or seeking a job that rests on knowledge you have not obtained will waste time for both you and an employer.

In most cases, technical support representatives and computer technicians of many types enter marketing and better-paying positions after several years' experience in other areas of the computer industry.

That can sound like the old "Which came first, the chicken or the egg?" story. It can be a strong temptation to complain, "How can I get experience unless someone hires me to give me that experience?"

The best answer is that there are entry-level jobs within the industry that may not be what you are looking for but that will give you a more rounded background as well as putting you in a position to move up the career ladder. You may, for instance, work first as a data entry operator or trainee, a distribution clerk, tape library attendant, peripheral equipment operator, or data control clerk. Some of this type of work may be a spin-off from computer training classes. Perhaps you may even be able to work for the community college itself. Short-term work through a temporary agency or at a summer or part-time job can be very helpful when it comes time to apply for your first full-time job.

With the rapidly growing popularity of the personal or home computer, which is sold through retail stores, it is reasonable to look for entry-level opportunities in computer marketing and service in that area.

Finding employment can seem baffling when you look for that first job. However, locating your first position requires multiple strategies. Job search techniques are a must. Several or all of the following should be considered and pursued.

Your closest, easiest contact is the school or college job placement office. In fact, the college placement office can be so valuable that you should check it out just as much as faculty and curriculum offerings. A good placement office may save you two or three years of career ladder training, according to reports of placement experts. The best time to begin making contacts with the placement office is early in your college career. Placement officers often can point you to valuable intern opportunities that will augment your classroom and lab studies.

Placement offices at many technical schools maintain computerized data bases for graduates. These are often used by employers nation-wide. Matching skills and needs, graduates and good positions is a source of pride to the institution. Take this advantage and make it work for you.

Visiting your local Chamber of Commerce may put you in touch with some prospective employers.

Another helpful move is to conduct information interviews. Ask for a fifteen-minute interview with a supervisor or manager of computer technicians. Your goal is to ask for guidance concerning entry into the field; it is *not* to ask for a job. Career ladders, preparation, employment trends, and local computer employer information are legitimate topics to discuss. Sooner or later, an information interview is likely to lead to a job offer.

Preparing Rèsumès and Writing Letters

Applying for a computer technician position is not like a friendly neighborhood sojourn. Knocking on doors or picking up the telephone is not likely to prove successful.

Many of the quality jobs may not even be located in your city or state. One up-to-date source of employment information is Computer Listings of Employment Opportunities (CLEO). For access information, call (213) 618-1525. CLEO was launched in California but is expanding its scope throughout the country.

Writing letters and résumés will be key to getting the job you want.

To catch the eye—and the interest—of a prospective employer, you need to explain quickly and clearly how you feel you can contribute to the success of the company. "This is what I can do," statements are the best way of getting noticed. In fact, selling yourself is the vital part of any job application process.

An application form is pretty cut and dried. It's straightforward and asks for vital statistics ranging from your name, address, and social security number to your education and experience data. It can easily give you the impression that all applicants are reduced to bare-bones, equal-approach information. That is not the whole story. Employers rarely if ever hire all applicants. They look for people who will do the job that needs doing. Knowing how to make yourself stand out of the crowd will pay off.

Your letter and your résumé are the door-opening tools you need at this point. They may not be the tools you are most comfortable with; after all, you have a technical mind and aptitude with your hands, or you wouldn't be considering this field. But some important thinking and planning are integral to the position you are seeking, and there is no better way to prove your qualifications than by applying your best thinking and planning to the job-seeking process.

What is your career objective?

That is, perhaps, your single most important piece of information as you prepare your résumé. It is important to you, and it is important to your future employer.

Thinking through the answer to this question will force you to analyze your strengths, your growth to this point both in education and in any previous jobs, and what kind of work you really want to do. You will find out a lot about yourself and your goals if you invest sufficient time and thought.

Once you know your career objective, you can begin organizing information about yourself that will illustrate your readiness to pursue that career.

When completed, your résumé should be neatly typed. It should look as professional as you can make it. If necessary, a friend, a relative, or a typing service should be enlisted to prepare the final copy.

Your résumé should be brief and to the point. One page should do it. On the first few lines, you should include your full name, address, telephone number, and your career objective. You may want to include your birth date, sex, and marital status, although new laws on fair employment practices make it unnecessary for you to do so.

Education and employment records are a significant part of the résumé. Special accomplishments and other interests may also be listed in order to put your best feats forward. Putting "sell" in your résumé will not only get you noticed but also increase your own confidence in your ability to do the job.

You should write an individual letter to each person receiving your résumé. The letter should be addressed to the person by name if at all possible. (You can call the company and ask the receptionist or switchboard operator for names, titles, and spellings.)

In the cover letter, you should ask for an interview, stating briefly your qualifications and what you can do for the employer.

Getting an interview is your primary purpose at this point. The interview is your opportunity to be a "live" résumé and to present your best self.

Keep your résumé and your letter positive. Never lie or misrepresent any information about yourself, but select your facts to promote interest in yourself. Remember, you want to catch the attention of a busy employer. You do not want to give that employer a reason for rejecting you.

Résumés are tools in the hands of employers—tools of both selection and elimination. That is scary for the applicant. It creates anxiety for many job seekers. Waiting for a response is also an anxious period. In many fields, applicants must blitz a great number of companies in order to get a few responses. In a high-demand field such as computer technicians, you may not have to take that approach if you are well prepared and if you research carefully before sending your letters and résumés.

Remember that employers in the computer industry are futurists. That means their outlook is somewhat different. With high technology changing things so rapidly, they exist in a world of change. They may not always know exactly what they want in a worker. Often they depend on schools and previous employers to screen out unqualified workers. However, they are looking for capable, qualified, skilled, dedicated workers who have captured some measure of futuristic thinking. They are looking for employees who enjoy their work, bringing to it an assortment of interpersonal relationship attitudes that will offer the employer a good basis for investing in additional training of the employee.

Preparing for the interview is often overlooked. Try to anticipate the questions that will be asked and be prepared to respond. Too much spontaneity may not be in your best interest. During the interview you will be selling yourself. The secret is to demonstrate your interest, your ability, your follow-through, and your potential for getting along with co-workers.

You should also give thought to the questions you would like to ask the interviewer. Research the company before you apply and a bit more thoroughly before your interview. Know *why* you want to work for that particular company and be able to say why.

Remember, too, that your appearance will do some talking for you. Physical fitness resulting from good health and exercise will contribute to the impression that you are equipped to do a good job. So will a neat, well-groomed appearance. An employer's first impression of you is important. It is also significant to the employer's customers and clients. Your appearance talks for you. It can convey the message that your job and your future are important to you and that you are prepared to give your best effort. Your appearance can say, "I'm a capable person, worthy of your respect," or it can convey a slipshod attitude that leads to lost opportunity for both you and an employer. Don't underestimate the necessity for being well groomed and appropriately dressed. Many technicians wear white-collar office attire; that is certainly a good choice for an interview.

COURTESY DeVRY INSTITUTE OF TECHNOLOGY

Students learn quickly that good interpersonal skills are necessary in the technical world.

Keep in mind that some companies may not be right for you. Part of the interview process is to discover compatibility between present and future co-workers. Rejection seems tough, but you really may not want every interview to end with a job offer. What you really want to achieve is to locate the one best job for you.

Chapter **XII**

Advancement and Job Satisfactions

Career Advancement and Related Occupations

Computer maintenance personnel usually start work as trainees, generally after completing at least two years of college or technical training.

As a computer service trainee, you learn about the kind of equipment sold and/or serviced by your employer. As we have seen, you would learn in two ways: (1) studying at company-operated schools, training sessions, or seminars; and (2) working under the close supervision of skilled technicians. Your work would be directly concerned with customer relations and servicing, adjusting, and repairing computers and related equipment.

One or two years of working in a trainee status should qualify you to become a Customer Service Representative. You may first be assigned to work with peripheral or key-driven equipment. As you gain competence, you may begin work on computers ranging from relatively simple to highly complex installations.

As a Customer Service Representative, you have the opportunity to demonstrate your ability to repair computers and related equipment. Equally important, you are able to demonstrate human relations and leadership skills as well. As you show your supervisors by your work actions that you are competent with the machines and confident with the customers, your value to the company steadily increases. Two or three years' experience at that level should bring you to the threshold of another level.

At that point, more choices begin to open up.

You can advance into related areas such as account management.

COURTESY U.S. DEPARTMENT OF LABOR

A technician uses test equipment to diagnose computer malfunction.

Sorbus Service Division/MAI, for instance, reports that 90 percent of its field managers come from the ranks of its field engineers.

Or you can become highly specialized in maintaining one kind of equipment. Technicians who demonstrate superior abilities and take additional training may become specialists or troubleshooters, who then help other technicians diagnose difficult problems.

Another avenue of upward progress, sometimes called upward mobility, is to move into a supervisory position. This might be called Customer Service Engineer, although, as indicated earlier, actual titles vary considerably depending on employers and on the specific nature of the work.

In the capacity of Customer Service Engineer, you would direct the work of twelve or fourteen Customer Service Representatives. You would also act as part of the management team for an assigned geographic area. Opportunities of this kind are open to those with strong interpersonal skills and leadership ability. The same traits could also lead you into computer sales.

About now, you can begin to realize that computer technician careers are in little danger of becoming dead-end jobs. In our competitive society, many workers are seeking jobs that have opportunities for advancement or for variety and learning new skills. You are now exploring a career field that offers both.

Other computer careers that may begin to sound exciting to you at this point include systems design and analysis or other management careers. Opportunities may well be open to you in those areas, especially if you continue your education and obtain a bachelor's degree in electronic or computer engineering. As a general rule, the more ambition you have and the higher you want to climb, the more formal (and informal) education you need.

With each advance in technology, new jobs open up. Alert technicians may find themselves in the right place at the right time to take advantage of such an opportunity. Who you know, what contacts you make, and how much they respect your work and abilities become increasingly important. The most responsible jobs are generally filled from within because employers want those who have proven dependable.

Sometimes your own expertise can open up new possibilities. As you work on equipment, you may see ways to improve existing technology. You may develop a part or a system on your own as a hobby and then find that there is a need for it in the open market. Today's breakthroughs are often a result of yesterday's significant ideas, particularly in software and ways to make computer systems easier to understand and to use.

The desire to have one's own shop or business, to be one's own boss has always been present in American workers. There will probably be more self-employment in the future. A word of warning, however.

Of all new business enterprises started, about two-thirds disappear from the scene within five years. Almost half are gone within two years. That tells us pretty quickly that it is not easy for most people to set up their own business, mainly because of the many strict government regulations designed to protect consumers, the environment, and employees who may feel discriminated against. Bankers report that not having your heart in your business is the way to fail. So is looking for rewards such as prestige, independence, or security.

At the same time, the Small Business Administration (SBA) has many aids available ranging from pamphlets, information, and counseling to guaranteed business loans to help new businesses get started. More and more major corporations are relying on private consultants to accomplish special projects (another form of entrepreneurship). Franchises—local businesses associated with a larger group of similar businesses—are another approach that gives you the freedom of running your own business with more help and less risk than going it alone.

If the idea of having your own shop or business some day appeals to you, what is necessary for success?

Integrity is the number one requirement, according to SBA representatives. Also resiliency, a burning desire, willingness to put in long hours of work, and instinct or a "nose for business." Note especially the long hours of work. Workers who like to go home when the work day is over may not be anywhere near enthusiastic enough to work long extra hours instead. That's what the boss must do if success is to be realized.

So far we've talked here about computer service and repair jobs. We need to remember that thousands of technicians are working in industry in other capacities, and thousands more are needed.

Manufacturers of computers and computer peripherals employ technicians in their research and development labs. There you would make prototypes or first attempts at new design equipment. You would do the hands-on building that engineers and computer designers want to try out.

These R & D technicians are not limited to computer operations. Most major corporations are involved in the creation and manufacture of multiple products.

For instance, major corporations such as Honeywell report a real need for experts in specific fields—especially electronic design engineers, solid state and optical physicists, material scientists, chemists, computer scientists (hardware and software) and—are you listening?—technicians in each of those areas. The field of robotics, they say, has increased their need for mechanical engineers. They also need people who specialize in human factors engineering (making machines easy for people to work with).

Those careers may sound unrelated to our subject, but computers have become commonplace in each of them and Honeywell and other major corporations want men and women who can offer more than expertise in a particular science. They want employees (including technicians) who can do their work on the newest tools available—computers.

Imbedded computers—microprocessors *within* products—open still more need for technicians. For example, microprocessor-based environmental control systems make it possible for homeowners to pre-program a week's worth of heating and cooling to suit the time of day and day of the week. Combinations of computers and sensors allow operators to control acres of oil refinery or chemical manufacturing plants from a central, easy-to-use control console. Those examples give you just a small idea of how and why technicians will be working with computers in almost every major industry.

Again, however, there is a warning.

Industry leaders back up their need for employees with an observation that there is an ever-decreasing supply of the highly trained, experienced professionals needed by high technology companies. They see an increasing need for people with master's and doctoral degrees as the demand grows for more powerful and more complex integrated circuits, energy control systems, and computers.

The fact that you are reading this book signifies that you have more than a passing interest in computers and in your future. Planning ahead will pay off for you. The sooner you start putting your plans into action, the better prepared you will be. It's easier to accomplish any goal you choose, no matter how grand, if you start early and take one well-planned step at a time.

Advancement into a top-of-the-line, well-paying, interesting career can begin in grade school. Mastering mathematics and computer expertise early can give you a foundation to build on. Like riding the crest of an ocean wave, you can stay abreast of new technology if you start early, stay prepared, and stay with it.

As a computer technician, you can start young in an entry-level position. You can perfect your skills and choose a career path from choices that range from highly specialized hands-on practical technologies to the white-collar world of management, from sales to engineering, from small business to corporate structures. You can work at your chosen career, perfecting skills, while at the same time furthering your education—and your opportunities.

And no matter which choice you pursue, you can feel a genuine sense of accomplishment in your work because you are part of a pioneering industrial growth never before experienced in the history of the world.

You will be in the forefront of the Information Age. Computer management leaders point out that data processors are already facing the second revolution of their careers with the advent of the micro-personal-desktop computer. Each new surge in technology brings with it new opportunities.

Other types of professional certification should be considered by those who are looking to advance with the high-tech industry. One is certification by the Institute for Certification of Computer Professionals (ICCP).

Professional activity rests on high standards of skill and knowledge, confidential relationships with people served, established standards of conduct and practice, and the observance of an ethical code. Computer professionals have established such codes through the ICCP. Copies of the codes of ethics, conduct, and good practice are available from the ICCP. Annual CCP examinations are given in three areas of specialization: business programming, scientific programming, and systems programming. They are primarily for senior-level computer programmers, but they are open to others. Passing of an examination and acceptance of the ICCP codes of ethics, conduct, and good practice are required to receive the CCP. Among the standards expected from members are social responsibility (combating ignorance as it concerns information processing technology) and integrity (not knowingly claiming competence beyond what you can demonstrate). Confidentiality must be respected at all times. Although certification is not aimed at technicians or technologists, those interested in advancement should be aware of the ICCP standards.

Remember, too, never to close any career door unless or until you are absolutely certain you want it closed. Keep yourself open to all possibilities, because today's noninterest may be tomorrow's opportunity. That goes for co-workers and supervisors as well as actual job specializations. You will be growing. So will the industry. You want to keep all your advantages in good form so that they will work for you. An open mind and a good reputation are powerful tools when it comes to advancement possibilities.

Job Satisfactions and Rewards

The very nature of the United States speaks to pioneering. By world standards, ours is still a young country. The excitement of discovering the land, colonizing it, and moving westward are all very recent in world history.

Looking back, we can study the forward movements of history from the Stone Age to the Industrial Revolution. It's easier for most people to look backwards and see changes in retrospect.

Some, of course, capture a vision of the future and, even if they are not exactly sure where it is leading, are willing to go with it. They find excitement, challenge, stimulation, and opportunity in a given direction, and those qualities make life interesting for them. To be sure, daily life may still be filled with the nitty-gritty, with small, routine chores. But the ability to see and feel a part of a genuine forward movement of history does carry internal satisfactions. The potential rewards of this kind of thinking should not be underestimated.

The impact that increased use of computers and their computing power will have is real. It is not a fad. It is not just one more step in progress. The Information Age is upon us. This electronic, supersonic world is unique in history.

Some estimate that by 1985 as much as 75 percent of all jobs will involve computers and technical specialization. Even if that estimate should prove high, it clearly indicates the wave of the future.

The skills needed are not easily or quickly learned—little of real value ever is—but mastery of modern skills will equip you for a modern world.

On a personal level, it is true that job satisfaction involves feeling that your work is worthwhile and that it is achieving a real purpose. A United States President once emphasized that every person needs to feel part of a cause larger than himself or herself. A feeling of contributing to history and to other people who are carrying out valuable functions cannot be underestimated. This kind of feeling is strongly motivating. With motivation come enthusiasm, pride, accomplishment, and a sense of being worthwhile. With those feelings come commitment to your work and a belief in yourself and what you are doing.

In the daily routines of life, variety does add interest. A computer service technician who daily travels to different locations, coming into contact with new and different people and tasks, also experiences a bit of the outdoors as part of the routine. A bench technician whether in repair or industry, on the other hand, finds variety in a different way— in the challenges of increasingly complex technology. Both, of course, are working with new and constantly changing technology.

As the American way of life is continually geared to change, workers find that over a period of years they become bored if they are forced into a routine mold. Life can become very gray. Workers can become listless and less productive. They refer to their jobs as "dead-end."

Entering a pioneering field as it is exploding with new knowledge and a vast need for growth and new workers gives you an almost unprecedented opportunity to grow with the industry. Computers and high technology are exploding now in unprecedented ways.

According to Edward A. Faber, president of Computerland, the year 1982 will be considered the real dawning of the home uses of computers. That was the year when individuals and small businesses began to have access to the same computerized capability as large corporations. That access is proving to be a lifesaver for small business. Computers themselves were not new, but as they became cheaper and smaller, they became more accessible to the mass market. That is what is causing revolution, according to Faber. He sees the next real breakthroughs in the creation of more data bases and in the elimination of the keyboard; the latter refers to the ability to use verbal commands, a possibility that is mind-boggling.

Growing Opportunities

It is important to realize that new workers must enter at the entry level. It is equally important to realize that promotions, opportunities to grow and to learn, career changes, and being in the right place at the right time for jobs that may not even be recognized yet—all add up to a job outlook that can be continually rewarding. There is little chance of being caught in a dead end if you are working with computers.

Data collected by the U.S. Department of Labor in 1980 shows that technicians have a strong attachment to their occupation. The number of workers choosing to leave the ranks of technicians is one of the lowest among all types of workers. Only one computer service technician in 20 transferred to a different occupation, a proportionately small number that indicates the satisfaction most technicians find in their work.

Another significant statistic is that relatively few computer technicians suffered unemployment—only about 1 in 100. That pattern is attributed to the fact that it is a rapidly growing field that offers many opportunities for advancement, high earnings, and good working conditions.

It is also interesting to note that there are few retirements in the field—about 2 in 100—which reflects a younger average age in this relatively new occupation. Six of every 10 openings for computer service technicians in 1980 were filled by workers in their mid to late twenties who had worked for several years in another occupation that also required knowledge of electronics and that provided a working background for the job of computer service technician. The background careers included business machine repairer, television service technician, and engineering technician.

Another aspect that would contribute to your feeling of satisfaction would be your recognition of the relationship between high-tech and high-touch. Some aspects of the computer world, with its sterile high technology, must be combined with high-touch or interpersonal, in-touch-with-nature activity. An ideal balance is highly important, both for society and for you as a person. Increasingly, you will find that employers build in some aspect of interpersonal contacts. They are beginning to realize the importance of maintaining a balance. But you may also contribute to your own healthy balance by cultivating leisure time activities that get you outdoors in touch with nature and in touch with people. Ideally, such activities should be different from your technical work. They should complement your highly technical, machine-interactive, sedentary work.

Any way you look at it, the computer and business equipment industry is one of the fastest-growing industries in the world. Continuing to be more challenging year after year, the information industry is projected to be the largest of all industries by the year 2000.

We already have some solid clues as we look at that prediction. Between 1960 and 1975, while other jobs were declining, computer and business equipment careers doubled.

The significant factor to note is that the sophistication of computer careers calls for highly qualified workers.

Highly qualified means being prepared.

That can be your starting point, your entrance into the wonderful world of tomorrow.

Colleges and Schools

Schools with Two-year Technology Programs
(Computers/Electronics)

ARIZONA
  Yavapai College, Prescott

ARKANSAS
  University of Arkansas, Little Rock

CALIFORNIA
  Cogswell College, San Francisco
  El Camino College, Via Torrance
  Evergreen College, San Jose
  Foothill College, Los Altos Hills
  Los Angeles Harbor College, Los Angeles
  Los Angeles Trade Tech College, Los Angeles
  Mount San Antonio College, Walnut
  Saddleback College North, Irvine
  San Bernardino Valley College, San Bernardino
  San Jose City College, San Jose
  San Mateo College, San Mateo
  Santa Monica College, Santa Monica
  Ventura College, Ventura

COLORADO
  University of Southern Colorado, Pueblo

CONNECTICUT
  Hartford State Technical College, Hartford
  Norwalk State Technical College, Norwalk
  Thames Valley State Technical College, Norwich
  Waterbury State Technical College, Waterbury

DISTRICT OF COLUMBIA
University of the District of Columbia, Washington

FLORIDA
Miami-Dade Community College, Miami

GEORGIA
Southern Tech, Marietta

IDAHO
Ricks College, Rexburg

ILLINOIS
Harper College, Palatine
Illinois Central College, East Peoria
Rock Valley College, Rockford
Wilbur Wright College, Chicago

INDIANA
Indiana State University, Terre Haute
Indiana University-Purdue University, Fort Wayne
Indiana University-Purdue University, Indianapolis
Purdue University, Hammond

IOWA
Hawkeye Institute of Technology, Waterloo

KANSAS
Hutchinson Community College, Hutchinson

MASSACHUSETTS
Wentworth Institute of Technology, Boston

MICHIGAN
Detroit Enginering Institute, Detroit
Henry Ford Community College, Dearborn
Jackson Community College, Jackson
Lake Superior State College, Sault Ste. Marie
Montcalm Community College, Sidney
Muskegon Community College, Muskegon

MINNESOTA
St. Cloud State University, St. Cloud

MISSOURI
Central Missouri University, Warrensburg
St. Louis Community College at Florissant Valley, Ferguson
Southwest Missouri State University, Springfield

NEBRASKA
Southeast Technical Community College, Milford
University of Nebraska, Omaha

NEW JERSEY
County College of Morris, Randolph

NEW MEXICO
New Mexico State University, Las Cruces

NEW YORK
Broome Community College, Binghamton
Erie Community College, Williamsville
Hudson Valley Community College, Troy
Mohawk Valley Community College, Utica
New York City Community College, Brooklyn
Orange City Community College, Middletown
State University of New York, Alfred
State University of New York, Farmingdale
Suffolk County Community College, Selden

NORTH CAROLINA
Forsyth Technical Institute, Winston-Salem
Gaston College, Dallas
Rowan Technical Institute, Salisbury
Wilson County Technical Institute, Wilson

OHIO
University of Akron, Akron
Cincinnati Technical College, Cincinnati
Cuyahoga Community College, Cleveland
Lorain County Community College, Elyria
Sinclair Community College, Dayton
University of Toledo, Toledo
Youngstown State University, Youngstown

PENNSYLVANIA
Pennsylvania Institute of Technology, Upper Darby

TEXAS
Texas State Technical Institute, Waco

WASHINGTON
Highline Community College, Midway

WISCONSIN
Gateway Technical Institute, Kenosha

Trade and Technical Schools

ARIZONA
   Arizona Tech, Phoenix

CALIFORNIA
   Control Data Institute, Anaheim
   Control Data Institute, Los Angeles
   Control Data Institute, Montclair
   Control Data Institute, San Francisco
   Control Data Institute, Woodland Hills
   National Technical Schools, Los Angeles

CONNECTICUT
   Porter and Chester Institute, Enfield
   Technical Careers Institute, West Haven

FLORIDA
   Miami Technical Institute, Miami
   Tampa Technical Institute, Tampa

GEORGIA
   Control Data Institute, Atlanta

ILLINOIS
   Control Data Institute, Bensenville
   Control Data Institute, Chicago
   DeVry Institute of Technology, Chicago
   Illinois Technical College, Chicago

IOWA
   Hamilton Technical College, Davenport

KANSAS
   Wichita Automotive and Electronics Institute, Wichita

MARYLAND
   Arundel Institute of Technology, Baltimore
   Control Data Institute, Baltimore

MASSACHUSETTS
   Associated Technical Institute, Woburn
   Control Data Institute, Burlington

MICHIGAN
   Control Data Institute, Southfield

MINNESOTA
  Brown Institute, Minneapolis
  Control Data Institute, Minneapolis
  Control Data Institute, St. Paul
  Dunwoody Industrial Institute, Minneapolis
  Northwestern Electronics Institute, Minneapolis

MISSOURI
  Basic Institute of Technology, St. Louis
  Ranken Technical Institute, St. Louis

NEW JERSEY
  Brick Computer Science Institute, Brick
  Lincoln Technical Institute, Pennsauken
  The Plaza School of Drafting, Paramus
  Union Technical Institute, Eatontown

NEW YORK
  Advanced Training Center — Kenmore Branch
  Advanced Training Center, Tonawanda
  Albert Merrill School, New York
  Control Data Institute, Garden City
  Control Data Institute, New York
  Island Drafting & Technical Institute, Amityville
  PSI Institute, New York
  SCS Business & Technical Institute, New York
  Suburban Technical School, Hempstead

OHIO
  Control Data Institute, Independence

PENNSYLVANIA
  Electronic Institute, Harrisburg
  Electronic Institute, Pittsburgh
  Lincoln Technical Institute, Allentown
  Lyons Technical Institute, Philadelphia
  R.E.T.S. Electronic Schools, Broomall

TEXAS
  Control Data Institute, Dallas
  Control Data Institute, Houston

VIRGINIA
  Control Data Institute, Arlington
  Electronic Computer Programming Institute, Norfolk

WISCONSIN
Control Data Institute, Milwaukee

Accredited Home Study Schools

Cleveland Institute of Electronics, Inc.
1776 East 17th Street
Cleveland, OH 44114

Heathkit/Zenith Educational Systems
Hilltop Road
St. Joseph, MI 49085

International Correspondence Schools (ICS)
Scranton, PA 18515

McGraw-Hill Continuing Education Center
3939 Wisconsin Avenue NW
Washington, DC 20016

National Radio Institute (NRI)
3939 Wisconsin Avenue NW
Washington, DC 20016

Helpful Organizations

American Association of Engineering Societies
345 East 47th Street
New York, NY 10017

American Federation of Information Processing Societies
1815 North Lynn Street St. 800
Arlington, VA 22209

American Society for Information Science
1010 16th Street NW
Washington, DC 20036

American Society for Engineering Education
Eleven Dupont Circle
Washington, DC 20036

Association for Computing Machinery
11 West 42nd Street
New York, NY 10036

Computer & Business Equipment Manufacturers Assn.
311 First Street, NW
Washington, DC 20001

ComputerTown (TM)
People's Computer Co.
P.O. Box E
Menlo Park, CA 94025

Institute for Certification of Computer Professionals
35 East Wacker Drive
Chicago, IL 60601

Institute of Electrical & Electronics Engineers, Inc.
345 East 47th Street
New York, NY 10017

IEEE Computer Society
1109 Spring Street
Silver Spring, MD 20901

Society of Manufacturing Engineers
One SME Drive, P.O. Box 930
Dearborn, MI 48128

Special Libraries Association
235 Park Avenue South
New York, NY 10003

State Departments of Education

State Employment Development Departments

Publications

Computer Publications

Byte
  70 Main Street
  St. Peterborough, NH 03458

Computers & Electronics
  One Park Avenue
  New York, NY 10016

Computerworld
  Box 880
  Framingham, MA 01701

Data Communications
  1221 Avenue of the Americas
  New York, NY 10020

Electronic News
  7 East 12th Street
  New York, NY 10003

Electronics
  1221 Avenue of the Americas
  New York, NY 10020

Electronics Test
  1050 Commonwealth Avenue
  Boston, MA 02215

Information Systems News
  333 East Shore Road
  Manhasset, NY 11030

Micro-Discovery
  5152 Katella Avenue, St. 102
  Los Alamitos, CA 90720

Mini-Micro Systems
  221 Columbus Avenue
  Boston, MA 02116

Personal Computing
  P.O. Box 2942
  Boulder, CO 80322

Personal Software
  50 Essex Street
  Rochelle Park, NJ 07662

Radio-Electronics
  200 Park Avenue South
  New York, NY 10003

Software News
  5 Kane Industrial Drive
  Hudson, MA 01749

Trade Journals

Note: New computer journals and magazines are proliferating. You will find many others that may meet your needs. Before subscribing, you should read several copies to be sure that a particular choice will meet your needs.

Glossary of Computer Language

Every career or discipline has a language of its own. That goes for the world of computers, too.

Learning the language at the outset of your interest will prove valuable. Knowing the correct words and the descriptive words gives you greater command of the technical nature of the computer world. Some words or acronyms are a kind of shorthand, allowing you to converse more easily without resorting to lengthy strings of technical words.

A good computer dictionary is a worthwhile investment. It may not sound any more interesting than a telephone directory, but reading a computer dictionary is one way to teach yourself a thing or three. Once you're at ease with computerese, you will begin to feel confident.

In the meantime, the following glossary will get you started.

acoustic coupler Molded rubber connector that makes it possible to attach a telephone handset to a computer. Computer information then can be transmitted, through the use of tones, over telephone lines to communicate with other computers. Stores of information may be transmitted rapidly and easily in this manner.

actual machine language (AML) Program written in the machine's code, requiring no translation.

alphabetic field Data that contains only letters and blanks.

alphanumeric Consisting of letters, digits, and/or special characters such as punctuation marks or mathematical symbols.

analog computer Computer designed to operate directly on continuous voltage. It represents numbers by continuous quantities, by mechanical quantities, or by models.

application Task that can be accomplished by using a computer. Examples include learning to type, word processing, playing games, solving math problems, monitoring energy uses, or building a budget. Application software contains the instructions necessary to set the function in motion.

array   List of numbers or strings (or other entities in more sophisticated systems). Various elements can be referred to by their position in the list. This method of keeping data in order allows the computer program to locate the information it needs to perform a task.

artificial intelligence   Field of computer science. Trying to make computers solve problems the way humans do is a step in trying to make computers intelligent in their own right. Computers as we know them do not "know" anything on their own, any more than a TV set knows what we want to view.

ASCII   *A*merican *S*tandard *C*ode for *I*nformation *I*nterchange, list of switch positions corresponding to each standard symbol. Pronounced "askey," the code standardizes the systems by which computer keyboarding produces the desired letters, numbers, and symbols. Computers differ from typewriters in that no precise character strikes a ribbon and makes its imprint. Computers print through a different pattern of bits for each letter, number, or symbol. Computer makers have agreed on the standard ASCII code for the sake of uniformity.

assembler   Program that translates assembly language into the computer's native language. Assembly language is more difficult for us to learn than BASIC, yet it enables the computer to operate faster and more powerfully. Most people do not need to learn assembly language; an assembler converts it to a language that is more usable.

backup tapes or disks   Copies of the master file (data/program files), used for recovery purposes. These spare copies prevent total loss of information in the event of a disk or computer crash.

BASIC   Acronym for *B*eginner's *A*ll-Purpose *S*ymbolic *I*nstruction *C*ode, a widely used symbolic programming language that can be used with almost all personal computers. It was invented by Kemeny and Kurtz at Dartmouth College in 1963.

batch processing   The processing of data in collections or groups, holding it until an appropriate time is determined for a computer production run.

baud   Measure of the speed with which information can be communicated between two devices. Technically, it is the number of bits transmitted or received per second. If the information is, for example, in the form of alphabetic characters, then 300 baud corresponds to about 30 characters per second.

binary   System of counting numbers in which each digit stands for a power of two. (In the decimal system, each digit stands for a multiple of a power of 10.) The computer's memory is primitive and understands only two states (as a switch knows only on and off). Even letters of the alphabet and punctuation marks are translated into 1's and 0's before being used by the computer and then translated back into English when we need to see the results. Understanding binary numbers is not crucial when using personal computers because the computer does it all.

binary number   Number with a combination of 0's and 1's. It is ideally suited for use with computers where 0 represents "off" and 1 represents "on."

BIT   *B*inary dig*it*, a single element of a binary number with a value of 1 or 0. A bit is the smallest amount of information that can be known.

bug   Error. A hardware bug is a malfunction or design error in the computer or its peripherals. A software bug is a programming error.

bulletin board   Increasing numbers of people are using computers as electronic bulletin boards. By dialing an appropriate telephone number, computer users of shared interests are able to read or leave messages. Advanced uses include private electronic mail, free software, ongoing conferences, and access to large collections of public information.

bus   Pathway that electrical signals follow inside the computer, a route by which information is delivered. A bus can carry a complicated series of electrical signals without getting them mixed up.

byte   Sequence of eight bits used to represent a character in storage in the computer. In practice, a byte usually represents an alphanumeric character or a number in the range 0 to 255.

cable   Enclosed group of wires used to connect computers and peripherals.

cathode ray tube (CRT)   Terminal with a display screen similar to a television screen. Also called a *monitor*.

central processing unit (CPU)   The "brains" of the computer system, the CPU controls the computer's operation—input, data transfer, arithmetic, logic, and output.

character   Single unit—a letter, digit, or special symbol.

chip   Small (typically less than half a centimeter on a side and quite thin) piece of material (usually silicon) into which have been formed circuit elements ranging from a few dozen to tens of thousands. A chip is made by etching the material, depositing microscopic metal conductors, and selectively impregnating ("doping") the material with various elements that change its properties. The microscopic bit of silicon is actually grown chemically in layers and etched until it becomes an integrated circuit that forms the heart of a microprocessor.

COBOL   Acronym for *Co*mmon *B*usiness *O*riented *L*anguage, an Englishlike programming language best suited for business applications.

command   Request to the computer that is executed as soon as it is received.

communication lines   Telephone or teletype lines used in a teleprocessing system to link the terminals to the CPU.

compatibility   Software and peripherals must be compatible or able to interact with each other. Hardly anything that is designed for one brand or model of computer will work with another. Compatibility factors and knowing one's needs, therefore, are extremely important when selecting a computer.

compiler   Program that translates one computer language into another. Most commonly the term refers to a program that translates a higher-level language into the computer's native language. Programs that have been compiled operate faster and usually take up less space in the computer's memory.

computer   Machine that can receive and then follow instructions through the use of very fast electrical signals to manipulate information. In any computer, both the set of instructions and the information on which the instructions operate may be varied from one moment to another. The machine processes data automatically by electronic digital techniques and can handle text as well as numbers.

computer-assigned instruction (CAI)   Educational tool by which the computer and the user interact; the computer displays information and asks questions. Correct answers allow the user to proceed.

computerese   Dialect spoken and written by computer buffs; it seems to signify initiation into a new society.

computer operator   Person responsibible for feeding input into the computer, communicating with the CPU, and transmitting the output. The operator follows instructions or flowcharts for each program.

computer system   Group of devices, including hardware and software, that work together to make it possible to input information and receive useful results. A system includes various input, output, and storage devices.

CPU   (See *central processing unit.*)

CRT   (See *cathode ray tube.*)

cursor Symbol placed on the screen to let you know where the next character you type will appear.

daisy-wheel printer Type of printer that uses a circular wheel composed of individual spokes or petals, each carrying a single character. It is often called a letter-quality printer because its printed output is so similar to that of an electric typewriter. It is more expensive and usually slower than a dot-matrix printer.

data Collection of raw facts that are entered into the computer as input, processed, and transformed into meaningful information. Computer commands act on the information.

data base Collection of data, organized in a useful way.

data processing Operations required to change raw facts into useful information. It often refers to a professional level of applications programming used to work with payrolls, insurance claims, banking records, tracking income from multiple sources, etc.

debug To correct errors in a program.

digital Relating to separate and discrete "counting" numbers instead of continuously variable numbers.

DIP Acronym for *D*ual *I*n-line *P*ackage, the most common physical form for an IC, which has two rows of leads that look something like the legs of a caterpillar. See *integrated circuit*.

disassembler Program that translates a computer's native language into assembly language.

disk Circular piece of material that has a magnetic coating similar to that found on ordinary recording tape. It is round and usually encased in a dustproof cover. Digital information can be stored magnetically on a disk, much as musical information is stored on a magnetic tape. Disks are also sources of information from which the CPU can read instructions and data. Disks can be hard or floppy.

disk drive Peripheral that can store information on and retrieve information from a disk. If the disk is like a record, then the disk drive is like a record player. It is a highly efficient and speedy mechanism that actually writes on and reads from disks. It is also highly sensitive and can be damaged by almost invisible things such as cigarette smoke or fingerprints.

documentation Written information that describes a program or system in its entirety and comes with every piece of hardware and software. Careful reading of the documentation tells how to use the product, what guarantees are in effect, and what to do if something goes wrong.

DOS   Acronym for *D*isk *O*perating *S*ystem, a collection of programs that facilitate use of a disk drive. It is usually pronounced "doss."

dot-matrix printer   Fast, inexpensive printer that forms letters by making patterns of tiny dots. Quality may depend on the variety of typeface commands that it can use. Dot graphics are a feature of many dot-matrix printers.

editing   Making corrections or changes in a program or data.

EPROM   Acronym for *E*rasable *P*rogrammable *R*ead-*O*nly *M*emory, a memory in which the data pattern may be erased to allow a new pattern to be used. Some types use a transparent lid to expose the chip to ultraviolet light for erasure. The chip is supplied in the erased condition.

execution phase   The computer "run"—the operating cycle during which the program is being processed.

file   Collection of individual records that are considered as one unit.

floppy disk   Small inexpensive disk, called "floppy" because it is made from flexible materials, as distinct from "hard" disks, which are made from rigid materials.

flowchart   Visual symbolic pathway of the logic to be used with a program or system.

format (verb)   To specify the form in which something is to appear.

FORTRAN   An acronym for *For*mula *Tran*slator, symbolic programming language most suited for scientific, mathematical problems.

graphic   Visible as a distinct, recognizable shape or color. Graphics relate to drawings, charts, or illustrations.

hard copy   Permanent record on paper or other durable surface of computer output.

hardware   The physical parts of a computer system. Hardware must be plugged in, connected, and kept free of dust.

initialize   To set up the starting conditions necessary for the execution of the remainder of a program. To initialize a disk is to prepare it so that the computer can later store data on it.

input   Information entering the computer system for processing. The same data can be input one instant and output the next as it moves from one computer device to another. Generally, input devices include the keyboard, disk drive (or cassette tape recorder), graphics pads, lightpens, touch-sensitive display screens, and microphones.

interactive   Describing a computer system that responds to the user quickly—usually in less than a second for a typical action. All personal computers are interactive.

interface   The electronics that allow two different devices to communicate with each other; any situation in which two entities (for instance, a person and a computer) communicate.

interpreter (See *assembler*; *compiler*.)

integrated circuit (IC) Interconnected array of components fabricated from a single crystal of semiconductor material by etching, doping, and diffusion, and capable of performing at least one and sometimes many complete circuit functions.

I/O Abbreviation for Input and/or Output. Keyboards, disk drives, and printers are I/O devices.

joystick Plug-in multidirectional device usually used to play arcade-style games on microcomputers. It is also used for graphics.

K Kilo, which means 1,000 (or 1024). A computer with 32K bytes of memory has 32 times 1024 (or 32,768) bytes of memory.

language Set of conventions (commands) specifying how to tell a computer what to do. There are many languages such as BASIC, PASCAL, and FORTRAN.

load To enter instructions or data into a computer.

loop Steps in a program or flowchart to be done a fixed number of times.

machine language The native language of a particular computer; a binary language.

mainframe The heart of a large, powerful, full-scale business computer system. Many of today's personal computers are as powerful as the original mainframes.

megabyte One million bytes of storage.

memory Storage capacity of a computer system; the portion of a computer that stores information.

menu List of options from which to choose.

microcomputer Complete, small to medium-size desk-top computer based on a microprocessor.

microprocessor Small chip of silicon that electronically controls specific capabilities of computers and other machine equipment. The part that actually does the computing, it includes memory, I/O channels, and the CPU.

minicomputer Powerful general-purpose computer, smaller than a mainframe, larger than a microcomputer.

modem Abbreviation of the words *MO*dulator-*DEM*odulator, an electronic device used to connect computers and terminals over telephone lines (and other communication media). It operates by changing the digital information into musical tones (modulating) and from musical tones to digital information (demodulating).

modulator Device enabling a personal computer to use any ordinary television set for output. It is sometimes called an RF modulator. RF stands for Radio Frequency, although the actual hookup is with Television Broadcasting Frequency.

monitor   Specially manufactured display screen (CRT) or television screen used to view temporary images being processed by the computer.

native language   Language that a computer was built to understand but which may be inconvenient to use.

nibble   Between a bit and a byte; a piece of information that is four bits long.

numeric   Consisting of data composed entirely of numbers (may include a decimal point or hyphen).

on-line   Under the continual control of the main computer; having continual access to the main computer.

operating system   Group of control programs that permit the computer to work automatically. They tell the internal parts of a computer how to interact in a way similar to the functioning of traffic signals.

optical character recognition (OCR) device   Hardware that reads typed or handwritten documents for translation into computer-usable form.

output   Data that has been processed by the computer; information leaving a device or a process.

paddle   Plug-in device using a knob or dial to relay instructions to the computer. Paddles are used in some computer games or to lessen keyboard use.

parallel   Occurring at the same time. A parallel interface is one that controls a number of distinct electrical signals simultaneously.

PASCAL   Structured higher-level programming language.

peripheral   Device that can send information to or receive information from a computer. Typical peripherals are disk drives, printers, modems, television sets, and monitors.

personal computer   Microcomputer.

port   Opening or access on a computer through which a peripheral may communicate by means of an attached cable.

printer   Typewriterlike machine linked to the computer for the purpose of printing computer output on paper. A line printer prints a whole line at a time. A serial printer prints one character at a time.

program   Series of instructions to guide the computer as it reads input data, processes it, and converts it to output.

PROM   Acronym for *P*rogrammable *R*ead-*O*nly *M*emory.

prompt   Symbol that appears on the computer's display to let the user know it is ready to pay attention to commands.

RAM   Acronym for *R*andom-*A*ccess *M*emory, the main memory of any computer where information is stored temporarily by sections. The information in RAM is lost whenever the power is turned off.

ROM   Acronym for *R*ead-*O*nly *M*emory, a memory in which information is stored permanently, usually by the manufacturer, and cannot be changed.

RS-232   Common method agreed to by most computer equipment manufacturers for sending electronic data from one machine to another. It refers to the design of the plug, cable, and socket used to connect modems to microcomputers but is sometimes used in the printer connections as well.

RUN   Command given to a small computer that causes it to obey the program instructions in memory.

save   To store a program somewhere other than in the computer's memory, for example on a disk or cassette tape.

schematic   Electronic roadmap showing the interworkings of a computer or other electronic equipment from which a technician works. The diagram uses graphic symbols to show components and their connections as well as the values of the various parts. It permits the building or tracing of circuit and flow paths for continuity.

scroll   To move all the text on the screen (usually upward) to make room for more text (usually at the bottom).

sheet feed   Method of printing on a single sheet of paper at a time.

silicon   Chemical element of which most of today's tiny computer components are made. Powerful machines that used to fill entire rooms are now built on a single silicon chip the size of a postage stamp.

simulation   Type of computer program that represents a life situation; may be educational or recreational.

soft copy   Computer output that appears on the visual display but is not retained unless printed on paper by a printer.

software   Programs (instructions) that enable the computer system to operate by telling it exactly what to do; usually on disk or tape. Software varies in quality and in price, depending on the sophistication and complexity of the program and the follow-up support service involved.

storage   Memory device such as a disk where information may be entered, kept, and retrieved later.

string   Sequence of letters, numerals, and other characters; a specific sequence of items grouped in a series according to certain programming rules.

syntax   Rules that specify exactly how an instruction can be written.

telecommunication   Electronic transfer of information from one place to another.

teleprocessing   Use of telephone communication lines to handle the flow of data from remote terminals to a central computer center.

terminal   Typewriterlike device used to enter and receive data from the CPU.

text   Data other than numbers; a great many characters treated as a unit.

tractor feed   Method of printing on continuous sheets of paper separated by perforations and fan-folded. Holes in the margins of the paper are held in place by tractor teeth on the printer assembly.

user   The person operating the computer system.

users' group   Association of people who have an interest in a particular computer or group of computers. They usually meet to exchange information, share programs, trade equipment, and explore new computer uses.

utility   Software used by advanced computer programmers.

variable   Quantity or value that can assume any of the numbers of some set of numbers.

window   Portion of the computer's display that is dedicated to some special purpose.

word processing   Preparation of documents or printed material by use of the computer. Words may be typed, changed, stored, re-arranged, filed and retrieved, formatted, edited, and printed.

write protect   To prevent the loss of information on a disk by erasing or writing over it, a notch on the disk can be taped over. With that write-protected notch covered over, new information cannot be added and the previously recorded information is protected.